THEM… WITHIN US

Todd David Gross

BROADWAY PLAY PUBLISHING INC
224 E 62nd St, NY, NY 10065
www.broadwayplaypub.com
info@broadwayplaypub.com

THEM…WITHIN US
© Copyright 1994 by Todd David Gross

All rights reserved. This work is fully protected under the copyright laws of the United States of America. No part of this publication may be photocopied, reproduced, stored in a retrieval system, or transmitted, in any form or by any means, electronic, mechanical, recording, or otherwise, without the prior permission of the publisher. Additional copies of this play are available from the publisher.

Written permission is required for live performance of any sort. This includes readings, cuttings, scenes, and excerpts. For amateur and stock performances, please contact Broadway Play Publishing Inc. For all other rights please contact the author c/o B P P I.

Book design: Marie Donovan
Page make-up: Adobe Indesign
Typeface: Palatino

THEM…WITHIN US was initially mounted at the Edison Valley Playhouse, Phyliss Donato, Artistic Director, Rick Engler, Director.

THEM…WITHIN US was subsequently produced by M & J Entertainment Corporation, at the Theatre Row Theatre in New York City. It opened on 25 October 1992 with the following cast and creative contributors:

SUSAN/DEE .... Bonnie Black
ROGER/ENN .... Marcus Olson
TOMMY .... Steven Sennett
SARAH .... Marceline Hugot

Director .... Allan Carlsen
Set designer .... Ray Recht
Lighting designer .... F Mitchell Dana
Costume designer .... Chelsea Harriman
Sound designer .... Todd Gross, Bob Lazaroff
Production stage manager .... Lisa Ledwich
Sound operator .... Jed Miller

CHARACTERS & SETTING

SUSAN, *thirty years old, organized, well put together.*

ROGER, *thirty-two years old, easy-going, a bit self-centered. Uses humor to evade conflict.*

TOMMY, *twenty years old, enthusiastic, boisterous, manic-depressive type personality.*

SARAH, *thirty years old, chunky, not well groomed, makes her own clothes, wears hiking boots, "earth-mother-type", etc.*

ACT ONE: *The time is the present. A winter storm threatens. It is in the afternoon.*

ACT TWO: *A moment* before *the end of* ACT ONE.

Sound: The sound of this play is extremely important and therefore is included as a cast member. It should be used liberally, and with imagination. It announces the aliens' arrival and departure. It tells us what their momentary physical conditions are (stress, pain, fear, etc.), and in the end aids in our understanding of the psychic interactions that occur.

INTRODUCTION

THEM...WITHIN US is a comedy of manners. It combines the elements of a relationship play with the uplifting magic of science fiction.

The play explores the modern-day dilemma of keeping a love relationship vital and alive. It is the story of ROGER and SUSAN, whose relationship is falling apart. They go up to Vermont for one final weekend together to see if it can be saved. It is there that the mishap takes place, and they become inhabited by two alien beings who are as unprepared for this occurrence as they are.

PRODUCTION NOTES

Having set out to write a simple romantic comedy with a "sci-fi" twist, I inadvertently created an acting nightmare (or challenge as the case may be). THEM...WITHIN US is a play of "business", of acting technique. Much of the humor comes not from the written word but rather from the extraordinary behavior the circumstances of the play force upon the characters. It is therefore a play of process, and you will need all the rehearsal time you can manage—and then some.

I would urge that you look carefully at the stage directions. View them as a starting point, not an ending one, a thing to stimulate creativity, not retard it. THEM...WITHIN US has gone through an extensive development process and any short cuts the script can provide can only lead to greater creative development on the part of your production.

It should always be remembered that THEM...WITHIN US is a comedy first. Any impulses leading towards the melodramatic seem to hinder it. If stuck between a dramatic choice or a comic one, we have found that the comic seems to work better. In regard to this, the intention of the opening "fight" between ROGER and SUSAN, although clear in my mind, has always been problematic in its execution. If the characters dig in too deeply it becomes melodramatic or "whiney", which offsets the tone of the play. In my mind their fight is not about confrontation but rather about evasion. Although their words may lead to a face-off, they are deeply afraid of the resulting action it will require. There are certainly areas of "heat," but they should be chosen carefully and kept to a minimum.

During the course of the plays development, we found that the best way to flesh out the roles of DEE and ENN was to begin with a physical motion. By thinking of the aliens as coming from the *inside out*, and the humans returning from the *outside in*, a clear physical pattern can be created. Having established the expanding/contracting motion, voice comes next. Since DEE and ENN are elevated personae, existing on a higher intellectual and spiritual plane, squeaky or high-pitched voices do them a disservice. As noted in the stage directions, their tone should be lower in register, "the voice of intelligence", but not roboticized, for they have their own emotions, likes, and dislikes.

One final note: A play is not unlike a piece of music. If played at the wrong speed the whole thing can be thrown off. THEM…WITHIN US should be played with the speed and energy of farce.

Special thanks to: Joe Cohen, Sam Cohen, Jim Longo, Alice Goldsmith, Sheila Mathews, Robin McAlpine, Patrick Barnes, Aaron Newman, John Jinx, Jim Van Bergen, Richard Gross, Zelda Gross, Dr Beth Abrams, Bob VanDerveer, Arnold Chapel, Denise Perotte, Gordon Wiener, Richard Gomez, Nancy Kadri, Ron Kadri, Lisa Marmorato, Elise Dewsberry-Green, Cassandra Medley, Paul Pilliteri, and all those friends and fellow writers whose help and support were invaluable throughout.

ACT ONE

(The set is the interior of a one-room cabin in Vermont. Simply furnished, the cabin is a bit of a ramshackle affair. Although neat and clean, it has the quality of being put together with whatever was at hand at the time. The kitchen table and chairs are somewhat ungainly, made of thin logs that might have been left over from a fireplace. The bed protrudes from the wall at an awkward—45 to 80 degree— angle. It looks out of place, taking up too much room. Lying on top of the bed, spanning its length and width, are four thin wooden poles or tree branches. Joined at the center and rising up several feet above the bed, they form a pyramid. The bottom of each pole rests upon the respective corners of the bed. Across from the bed is a small sitting area with a small couch or a chair or two. The kitchen, sink, etc. are along the back wall with a window over the sink. The window curtain is closed but once opened it reveals a mountain view. There is a knock at the door.)

SUSAN: *(Off stage)* Tommy? Hello?

ROGER: *(Off stage. Louder knocking:)* Tommy? TOMMY! Anyone in there? I guess not.

SUSAN: Here, let's use the key. *(Door opens)*

ROGER: *(Off stage)* Are you sure this is the right place?

SUSAN: It's got to be. This *is* the third cabin on the left, and the key *was* under the mat. Hello?

(ROGER and SUSAN enter.)

SUSAN: ...No one's here.

ROGER: How can you tell? Is there a light switch?

SUSAN: *(She finds it. Lights up.)* There, that's better.

ROGER: HA! It is just like your brother *not* to be here.

SUSAN: Oh hush... Look, there's a note. *(Crosses to table)*

ROGER: Oh yeah?

SUSAN: Hummm, it's not Tommy's handwriting.

ROGER: What does it say?

SUSAN: "Dear Susan and Roger, Unfortunately Thomas and I—"

ROGER: Thomas?

SUSAN: "Unfortunately Thomas and I were called away to help a neighbor-in-need. But we should be back in an hour or two. There are organic foodstuffs in the refrigerator—"

ROGER: Organic food stuffs? *(Looks in refrigerator)*

SUSAN: "—and the bottle of wine on the table is home made containing no additives. I have heard so much about you both I am looking forward to meeting you in the flesh. Sincerely yours, Sarah and Thomas"... Sarah?

ROGER: Thomas? Are you sure we're in the right place?

SUSAN: It does seem strange.

ROGER: Nothing's strange when it comes to your baby brother.

SUSAN: I'm sorry if being here is going to make it harder for you, but you've raised Tommy just as much as I have.

ROGER: Yeah yeah, I know, you don't have to remind me.

SUSAN: This...person, must be what he was hinting about.

ACT ONE 3

ROGER: Ah yes, the something he wanted to share with us.

SUSAN: Oh god, what next? He's so damn impulsive. He goes from one extreme to another.

ROGER: Well, you have to admit this place looks a lot better than the last one we found him in. *(Moves to bookcase)*

SUSAN: I guess so.

ROGER: At least it's clean.

SUSAN: *(Moves to bed)* What do you think this is for? *(Pointing to pyramid)*

ROGER: Probably some sort of sexual device.

SUSAN: *(Smiling)* It is not. It's probably for a mosquito net or something.

ROGER: Not in light of these books.

SUSAN: What do you mean?

ROGER: *(Reading titles)* Reincarnation Now! Herbal Medicine. The Power of the Pyramids. I'm not sure but we may have a modern day witch, or maybe a sixties hold-over, on our hands.

SUSAN: Oh great. I can just imagine what she must be like.

ROGER: From what I've seen so far, I'd say she's probably like you…with hair.

SUSAN: With hair?

ROGER: Yeah, on her legs and armpits.

SUSAN: Oh Roger.

ROGER: Well that usually goes hand in hand with organic food stuffs. *(Moves to bathroom)*

SUSAN: I wouldn't know. *(Looking in cabinets)* Her shelves are very orderly, anyway.

ROGER: *(Screams, backing out of bathroom)* AHHHHHHHHHHHH!

SUSAN: *(Scared)* What?!

ROGER: There's soap and towels in the bathroom!

SUSAN: *(Punching him)* Oh, cut it out.

ROGER: Well anyway, this place is certainly a marked improvement over the last one we found him in.

SUSAN: *(Looking about)* It's kind of cozy really.

ROGER: Yes, I guess it is. *(Sighs, retreats within self. Is depressed.)*

SUSAN: *(Opening curtain over sink)* Oh! Look at this view!

ROGER: *(Not looking)* Yes…it's nice.

(SUSAN stands transfixed at the window, staring out.) Well… *(A beat)* I'll go get the suitcases.

SUSAN: *(Calling after him)* And bring in the Hershfield Sausages.

ROGER: I don't know why we had to bring them. *(Exits)*

SUSAN: Because you can't get them up here. And you know they're Tommy's favorite. *(Continues to stare out the window. Speaking to self:)* The mountains are so beautiful, it almost seems unreal… God, I'm so depressed…

(ROGER enters.)

SUSAN: It's starting to snow.

ROGER: I know. *(Puts suitcase down. A beat)*

SUSAN: Well…

ROGER: Well what?

SUSAN: Well…what do you think?

ROGER: *(A beat)* Susan, maybe what we need is a break.

ACT ONE

SUSAN: A break?

ROGER: A vacation from each other.

SUSAN: You don't think we can do this without taking drastic measures?

ROGER: It wouldn't be a drastic measure. It would be a testing of the waters.

SUSAN: But where would you go? We've lived together for six years. Where would you stay?

ROGER: I don't know. *(Shrugs)* How about the den?

SUSAN: That doesn't sound too practical to me.

ROGER: Oh look, it's—it's unimportant.

SUSAN: Well, for how long would you think?

ROGER: I don't know. A few weeks, six months maybe.

SUSAN: Six months? Forget it!

ROGER: Why not? If it's over between us we'll know it. And if not it could help us rekindle what we had.

SUSAN: Roger, you rekindle a fire by tending it. Not leaving it.

ROGER: Sometimes you need to clear your head so you can put things back into perspective.

(SUSAN *shakes head no.*)

ROGER: Look, I don't know why the hell we have to make a decision so quickly. I mean, out of nowhere you suddenly decide that we have to get married or break up?! We were going along fine as we were.

SUSAN: We were not going along fine. We were just going along...Roger, it's been six years. Don't you think we should know by now?

ROGER: Well—

SUSAN: I'll be thirty-one soon. You know I want to have a family. I can't afford to waste any more time.

We have to figure out what's wrong *now*. I don't want to wait another year or two only to find out I've got to start all over again. We set a deadline and we're going to stick to it! ...Oh Roger, you know I want this to work.

(ROGER *nods.*)

SUSAN: ...What's wrong? Are you just not interested anymore? Is that the problem? Do you no longer care?

ROGER: I care.

SUSAN: Oh Roger!

ROGER: I do. I mean, you know I care for you. I just, I'm just—

SUSAN: Bored.

ROGER: Well, I—

SUSAN: You're bored let's face it.

ROGER: Susan, what do you want from me? After all this time together, I know you better than I know myself... It's all become so predictable.

SUSAN: *(A beat)* Sometimes I think the only thing that's real for you anymore is the fiction you write.

ROGER: What's that supposed to mean?

SUSAN: I think you've got this Susan prototype tucked away inside your brain. You think you've got me all figured out. But I'm not a rock, you know. I change, I grow.

ROGER: I know.

SUSAN: No you don't! Things have stagnated, Roger, because you have.

ROGER: Why is it you're always looking to blame me? You're bored too.

SUSAN: Oh Roger, what's happened to us?

ACT ONE 7

ROGER: I don't know. *(Softly)* I don't know.

SUSAN: Somehow we've died on our feet... Do you still love me?

ROGER: Of course, but—

SUSAN: Then why isn't it working?

ROGER: I don't know.

SUSAN: Well, you'd better figure it out soon because by next week I'm gone. Do you understand? No break. No vacation. Gone!

ROGER: Ah, with the wind no doubt. *(Sings, from the Righteous Brothers, "You've Lost That Loving Feeling")* "Now she's gone, gone, gone, whoa—oh-ohhhh—"

SUSAN: —Oh stop it! Why the hell is this bed sticking out like this?!!!! *(Shoves it flush against the wall)* There, that's better... Listen, I didn't mean to snap at you before.

ROGER: I didn't mean anything either.

SUSAN: Kiss-kiss?

ROGER: *(A beat, then nods)* Kiss-kiss.

(ROGER *and* SUSAN *move towards one another. "Kiss-kiss" is an intimate game they play. Cheek to cheek, facing the audience they press against one another until just the sides of their lips touch, then they quick kiss twice in unison, i.e., Kiss—kiss.)*

SUSAN: Let's not let Tommy know there's trouble, okay? You heard how good he sounded on the phone.

ROGER: I know.

SUSAN: Its just until we see how he is.

ROGER: I know, and I agree. Besides, I really want to meet this "person" responsible for transforming our unstable, grungy little dope addict Tommy into a...I don't know what. I mean I hate to be a "Doubting Thomas" but—

SUSAN: Oh please, if you can't say anything nice.

ROGER: Just kidding dear.

SUSAN: ...I'm hungry.

ROGER: Me too.

(SUSAN *moves to refrigerator. Suddenly a strange sound, henceforth known as the Alien Sound, is heard for a brief moment. The sound is a humming-throbbing-rumbling sort of sound, out of the ordinary but* not *out of this world.* ROGER *and* SUSAN *just begin to notice the sound as it disappears.* ROGER *shakes, clears his ear, i.e., "I didn't really hear that, did I?")*

ROGER: ...So, what have we got?

SUSAN: I'm not sure. *(Taking out from refrigerator)* Some fruit... *(Smells)* Some cheese I think. Sprouts and... something.

ROGER: Something?

SUSAN: You decide. Animal or vegetable? *(Hands it to him. It is vaguely fetal-like in a jar of liquid.)*

ROGER: Oooo, I don't know. *(Hands it back)*

SUSAN: Here's some bread.

ROGER: Good. *(Picking up wine bottle)* You think it's safe to drink this?

SUSAN: Why not?

ROGER: The note said it was homemade, and god knows what your brother put in it. Or have you forgotten those brownies he cooked for us a few years ago? I think I was high for a month.

SUSAN: The note said it had no additives. *(Setting table)*

ACT ONE

ROGER: All right, we'll proceed with caution. Not a bad spread. Bread, fruit, wine, and cheese, and something.

(Suddenly Alien Sound is heard more intensely than before.)

SUSAN: What is that?!

(Sound level increases.)

ROGER: I don't know. *(Crosses to window)* I don't see anything. *(Moves to door)*

SUSAN: It sounds like a plane or something?

ROGER: *(Sound fades to silence as he opens door and looks out)* Nothing out here... Maybe it was an echo.

SUSAN: An echo?

ROGER: Sounds can do funny things in these mountains. *(Checks behind the refrigerator. For added humor, perhaps he then opens it and listens.)* Still, that was pretty strange. For a moment it, it felt like it was all around us.

SUSAN: What do you mean?

ROGER: I don't know.

SUSAN: Don't scare me.

ROGER: Forget it. I'm sure it was just an echo... Come on, let's eat.

SUSAN: *(Pouring wine)* Here. Take your glass.

(ROGER takes it and smells it.)

SUSAN: What are you doing?

ROGER: Smelling it.

SUSAN: Oh come on.

ROGER: Better safe than sorry. Besides, it reminds me of something.

SUSAN: What?

ROGER: I don't know.

SUSAN: Well, is it all right?

ROGER: I think so.

SUSAN: Good.

ROGER: Here's to good fortune. Yours, mine, and theirs.

(ROGER *raises his glass with a flourish.* SUSAN *does same. He pretends to be about to drink his drink.* SUSAN *does the same. They both stop just short of drinking.*)

ROGER: Good fortune!

(ROGER *and* SUSAN *raise glasses again.*)

SUSAN: Good fortune!

(ROGER *and* SUSAN *both repeat motions of before, just stopping short of drinking.*)

SUSAN: Well, go ahead.

ROGER: Ladies before gentlemen. *(With a flourish)*

SUSAN: Age before beauty. *(Mimicking his flourish)*

ROGER: He's your brother.

SUSAN: I'm sure it's fine.

ROGER: So?

SUSAN: So?

ROGER: All right, we'll do it together.

SUSAN: No tricks.

ROGER: No tricks.

SUSAN: If you fake it I'll know.

ROGER: I won't, I promise.

SUSAN: Okay.

(ROGER *and* SUSAN *watch each other carefully.*)

ROGER: One.

SUSAN: Two.

ACT ONE

ROGER & SUSAN: *(Simultaneously)* Three! *(Both drink.)*

SUSAN: Hmmmm, not bad.

ROGER: It's kind of strong.

SUSAN: But good...I think it's just wine.

ROGER: Let's hope so. *(A beat)* A meadow!

SUSAN: What?

ROGER: Or a golf course. I don't know why but for some reason it reminds me of a golf course.

SUSAN: Roger, try the bread, it's very good.

ROGER: Hummm, yeah it is.

SUSAN: It's definitely homemade.

ROGER: *(Worried)* Oh? *(Takes a big drink of wine. A beat)* Hey, I've got an idea. We've probably got some time before they get back.

SUSAN: Yeah?

ROGER: Why don't we polish off this bottle and then maybe take a nap?

SUSAN: A nap? *(With sexual anticipation)*

ROGER: *(Yawns)* Yeah, all this fresh mountain air has made me tired.

SUSAN: If you want... *(Sighs)* Remember how we used to have fights for days?

ROGER: Ah yes, the bad old days.

SUSAN: Somehow I miss them.

ROGER: Hey look, we don't have to sleep the whole time. We could engage the warp drive if you like.

SUSAN: Yes we could...but I wish you wouldn't ask. I wish you'd just do it sometimes.

ROGER: Susan, we are not children, we're adults. We know what tomorrow brings. *(A beat as he experiences a rush from the wine. He rests his hand on the table.)* Whew, I'll tell you what else tomorrow's gonna bring, a hangover. I've already got a buzz from this stuff.

SUSAN: Me too, a little.

ROGER: It's really strong. You don't think that—

(ROGER stops in mid-sentence as sharp Alien Sound is heard. It pops his hand up off the table, stopping the moment his hand is off! He leaps back out of his chair.)

ROGER: —AH! What the hell?!!

SUSAN: What?

ROGER: Did you see that?

SUSAN: What?

ROGER: The table. My hand. The whole table started buzzing.

SUSAN: I didn't see anything.

ROGER: And my hand, it felt like it was being repelled. Like two magnetic poles of the same charge. Do you know what I mean?

SUSAN: Sort of.

ROGER: I've never felt anything like that before. Jesus, that was strange!

SUSAN: Are you all right?

ROGER: Yes, of course. I—

(Alien Sound. His hand pops off the table again. Sound off as before)

ROGER: AH! There! It happened again! Here, you feel it.

SUSAN: No, that's okay, I believe you.

ROGER: *(Taking her hand)* No no no come on.

SUSAN: Roger, I don't want to I—

ACT ONE 13

(SUSAN *places her hand on table and it is repelled with Sound as above. Scared.*)

SUSAN: Oooo! What is it?

ROGER: I don't know. Some sort of static electricity or something.

(*Rumbling sound is heard, added to Alien Sound. Dishes begin to rattle.*)

SUSAN: Oh my god, what's happening?!

(*As scene progresses Sounds get louder and louder, building to a crescendo.*)

ROGER: (*Rushing to window*) I don't know!

SUSAN: Is it an avalanche?

ROGER: I don't see anything.

SUSAN: An earthquake?

ROGER: I don't know.

SUSAN: Roger! Something's got me!!! I—I (*She begins to shake.*) AHHH! AHHH! AHHH! AHHHHHHHHHH!

ROGER: (*Runs to her*) SUSAN! I—it's—it's got me!

(ROGER *begins to shake.* ROGER *and* SUSAN *are standing side by side downstage center, facing the audience.*)

ROGER: AHHH! AHHH! AHHH! AHHHHHHHHHH!

(ROGER *and* SUSAN *both shake violently as Sound builds. It eventually drives them down to the floor where they collapse, one falling left and one falling right. They are rendered unconscious. [In this position, when they sit up, they will be beside one another and the audience's focus will not be split.] The Alien Sound recedes until only a low continuous hum is heard. They now glow or are cast in a different light—whatever. Eyes open. In voices that are qualitatively different from* ROGER *and* SUSAN, *lower in register, more articulate or classical, "the sound of intelligence," but NOT*

ROBOTICIZED. *Neither moves throughout scene until specified.)*

ROGER/ENN: *(Breathy at first, as though coming from a great distance)* Dee.

SUSAN/DEE: *(Same as above)* Enn.

(A pause)

ROGER/ENN: We...are here.

(A beat)

SUSAN/DEE: This...does not feel like Altion Ten. *(Beginning to panic)*

ENN: No.

DEE: *(Fearful)* Something is wrong!

ENN: I know.

DEE: *(A beat)* I am afraid!

ENN: And I... Do not move!

DEE: I remember...I...am blind, Enn.

ENN: I too cannot see.

DEE: I feel your presence.

ENN: And I yours. *(Humming sound begins to get louder)*

DEE: *(Sound surge. She groans in pain.)* ...Are you in pain?

ENN: It...intensifies.

(Sound level increases—no longer just a hum, it throbs faster and faster.)

DEE: There is much disturbance.

ENN: *(Groans in pain. Then both breathe quick short breaths and groan in pain.)* Dis—persion is increasing!

DEE: I AM DISSIPATING!!!!

ENN: AND I!!! EMERGENCY ONE!!!!

ACT ONE 15

DEE & ENN: *(They chant simultaneously. Sound is slowly reduced by their chant.)*
Within without, Chaos about,
Connect within, The center find.
The center find, Our space defined.
The center find, Our space definnnnnnnnnnnnnnn—

(DEE and ENN slowly rise to a sitting position with legs straight out in front of them. Their hum supercedes the Alien Sound, which by now is back to the original Hum. Otherwise, they still do not move.)

DEE & ENN: —nnnnnnnnnnnnnnnnnnnnnnnd. *(Both sigh.)*

DEE: Enn.

ENN: Dee.

DEE: It…subsides.

ENN: We are not yet focused.

DEE: Neither here—

ENN: —nor there.

DEE: What is happening?

ENN: Unknown. The Reperator…might have…failed to function.

DEE: But the tests proved true.

ENN: There were resistances at first.

DEE: Possibly this is a power fault?

ENN: Possibly… It seems my theory was correct.

DEE: Yes. The existence of an interlinking dimension—

ENN: Is proved…inadvertently by our presence here.

DEE: …So we are trapped.

ENN: Caught, interdimensionally.

DEE: And these bodies within which we are deposited—

ENN: Is that matter, in this dimension—

DEE & ENN: *(Simultaneously)* Which most resembles our own. *(A beat as they begin to "sense" themselves. What they are "exploring" is revealed to us through the motion of their arms. Since they are "neither-here-nor-there," their hands and arms never make physical contact with their bodies and therefore keep several inches away. It is a liquid motion, as though moving through water.)*

DEE: It is familiar.

ENN: *(A beat)* Primitive.

DEE: *(A beat)* Functional.

ENN: *(A beat)* I note the differences between us.

DEE: Yes. This is the Species Progenerator.

ENN: *(He moves hand up and down from crotch area—up and over the mountain—several times)* And this the Species Facilitator. Interesting how we have been translated even in this respect. Paralleling our mutual roles.

DEE: This body is in process!

ENN: *(Reaches towards her stomach area, which he "senses" from a distance.)* Yes…procreation is at hand.

DEE: I wonder if we affect its coding?

ENN: Unknown. But since we are not as yet locked in—

DEE: —No effect is probable.

(DEE and ENN begin to project themselves outwards, their arm motions becoming more global as they "sense" their way around the room.)

DEE: How long do you estimate our stay here?

ACT ONE

ENN: I do not know. Only a few moments if it is the Reperator. If there is a frequencer adjustment—

DEE: —Or a blockage.

ENN: Exx will have much to do to correct.

DEE: But if too long...

ENN: ...Yes. This was a possibility.

DEE: *(A pause)* This body is expressing undue amounts of surface fluid.

ENN: This one too. We must be generating great heat by our presence.

DEE: *(A surge of Sound, a sharp cry)* OOOO! *(Her body contracts violently.)*

ENN: OOOO! *(Same as above)*

DEE: These bodies could never sustain us.

ENN: No, they could not.

DEE: *(A beat)* If that is so and this be our end, these unfortunate creatures...

ENN: Join in our fate.

DEE: *(Pained)* Enn.

ENN: Dee.

DEE: It is violation.

ENN: Without intention.

DEE: Violation nevertheless.

ENN: We have time. These bodies are well constructed.

(Alien Sound changes from a hum to a pulsation. Both bodies begin to sway in a circular motion in time to the sound.)

DEE: What...is happening?!

ENN: I am not sure.

DEE: The frequency is...vacillating!

ENN: Hold on!

(As the speed of the pulsating Sound increases, DEE and ENN sway more quickly, making tighter circles until they are simply shaking once more.)

DEE: Enn!

ENN: Dee.

DEE: Forever mine?

ENN: Forever thine. *(Shaking is most violent)*

DEE: I...am...being...pulled!

ENN: Yes! It...must...be...

DEE & ENN: *(Simultaneously)* EXX!

(Pulsating Sound is overridden by continuous Alien Sound.)

ENN: We are—

DEE: —Receding.

DEE & ENN: *(Simultaneously)* Along the same path. *(Both down to floor)*

ENN: There must be a blockage in the frequencer.

DEE: If that is so—

ENN: —We may be returned here again.

(DEE and ENN recede. Sound fades to silence. A long pause.)

ROGER: *(Groans. Hoarse voice:)* Susan?

SUSAN: *(Groans. Hoarse voice:)* Roger?

(ROGER and SUSAN begin to move.)

ROGER: Are you all right?

SUSAN: I think so.

ROGER: My mouth...is so dry.

SUSAN: Mine too.

ACT ONE

ROGER: Thirsty. *(Crosses to sink, pours self a glass of water. Gulps it down)*

SUSAN: I'm so hot. *(Crosses to sink, taking off sweater)*

ROGER: Me too.

SUSAN: *(Drinking)* I feel like I've been locked in a sauna for a week. What happened?

ROGER: I don't know. *(Hands her water)* Here. *(To window)* The mountain's still there, so I guess it wasn't an avalanche.

SUSAN: An earthquake then?

ROGER: Not like any I've ever felt…I think it was your brother.

SUSAN: My brother?

ROGER: I think he spiked the wine.

SUSAN: I'm sure he didn't.

ROGER: Then how do you explain what happened?

SUSAN: I don't know.

ROGER: Did you ever feel anything like that before?

SUSAN: No.

ROGER: Me neither.

SUSAN: I can't believe he'd do that. Not after the last time. Besides, he was just a kid then.

ROGER: Hey, just because he's twenty years old now doesn't mean he's an adult.

SUSAN: Maybe it was a reaction to something we ate.

ROGER: Ah yes, the psilocybin swiss cheese.

SUSAN: Well, do you have a better idea?

ROGER: No. Still, where your brother is concerned—

SUSAN: I'm sure he wouldn't do anything to hurt us.

ROGER: No, I suppose not.

SUSAN: I know he wouldn't! ...It's very strange, though. During that awful noise I thought I heard voices, but they were coming from inside my head. Oh Roger, I'm frightened.

(ROGER *puts his arm around* SUSAN.)

ROGER: I know what you mean. It seemed the same to me. I'll speak to Tommy!

SUSAN: Okay, but don't be antagonistic.

ROGER: I won't.

SUSAN: And don't start with him right away.

ROGER: I'll be very tactful.

SUSAN: Okay... Hey, look at me.

ROGER: What?

SUSAN: You haven't been using my bronzing gel, have you?

ROGER: No, why?

SUSAN: You've got a lot of color in your face.

ROGER: Oh? Come to think of it, so do you.

SUSAN: Really? God, my face feels so dry. *(Goes to pocketbook)*

ROGER: Mine too.

SUSAN: I've got some skin moisturizer somewhere.

ROGER: This is all very strange.

SUSAN: Come here.

ROGER: I mean, I've never heard of anything like this.

SUSAN: Hold still. *(She applies moisturizer to his face.)*

ROGER: First we drink the wine.

SUSAN: Close your eyes.

ACT ONE

ROGER: Then we *think* the house starts to shake. We hear voices in our heads—

SUSAN: Close your mouth. Good. You're done.

ROGER: I'll do you. *(He applies some to her face.)* Then we have cotton mouth and now our faces are red like we've been sunburned. I'll tell you, to have a physical reaction like this it's got to be the wine.

SUSAN: Maybe it *was* the cheese.

ROGER: Come on, have you ever gotten high from cheese?

SUSAN: No. But maybe it's gone bad. Or maybe we had an allergic reaction to it.

ROGER: I don't know. But whatever it was, it was very strange.

(TOMMY's voice is heard coming towards the cabin, calling out, "They're here, they're here, I can't wait to see them, etc.")

SUSAN: That must be Tommy.

ROGER: I think we should say something.

SUSAN: All right. But not right away, okay? You know how sensitive he can be.

ROGER: All right. I know.

TOMMY: *(Off stage)* Hey you guys! *(A loud whistle)* Yahooooo! It's me! *(Knocks on the door)* Come on, open up! Or I'll huff and puff and blow the door down!

(SUSAN opens door and TOMMY comes bursting in.)

TOMMY: SUZY!!! *(He picks her up in a bear hug and twirls her around the room.)*

SUSAN: Tommy! *(Laughs)* Stop. Put me down, put me down.

TOMMY: It's so great to have you here. *(Putting her down, sees* ROGER*)* Hey Rog.

ROGER: *(Teasing)* Hello...Thomas.

TOMMY: How's it goin? *(Extends his hand)*

ROGER: Good. It's been a while.

*(*ROGER *reaches for his hand.* TOMMY *instantly twists* ROGER's *arm into a half nelson. This is a game they have played often when* TOMMY *was younger. A brief wrestling match ensues.)*

TOMMY: *(Like a wrestling announcer)* "And Hulk Hogan grabs San Martino in a Death Grip! AHHHHH— But he escapes

*(*ROGER *reaches back with his free arm and grabs* TOMMY *in a headlock and flips him over his hip.)*

TOMMY: and takes him down."

*(*ROGER *and* TOMMY *both go down.)*

SUSAN: Oh you two. Cut it out! Stop!

TOMMY: "And the crowd roars."

SUSAN: I'll fix you both. *(She leaps on top of them.)*

TOMMY: AHHHHHHH! "And the roof caves in, crushing them all!"

(They all laugh.)

SUSAN: Come on, get up.

TOMMY: *(Helping* ROGER *up)* Hey Rog. You outta shape or what? *(Laughs)* You look a little red in the face.

ROGER: Oh yeah? Well, I thought maybe you could shed a little light on the subject.

TOMMY: Whatta ya mean?

SUSAN: Oh, he's just kidding. *(Moving in between them)* Here, let me look at you. I swear you're still growing.

ACT ONE 23

And look at this. *(Touching his face)* When did you shave it off?

TOMMY: About six weeks ago. You like it?

SUSAN: Didn't I always tell you your face was too nice to hide behind all that hair?

TOMMY: *(Smiling)* Yeah. Sarah said the same thing—

SUSAN: Oh? That's nice.

TOMMY: —didn't you, Hon.

SARAH: *(Who has been standing just at the doorway, comes all the way in, shyly.)* Yes, I guess I did.

(SUSAN *and* ROGER *are surprised and a bit embarrassed.*)

SUSAN: Oh!

TOMMY: Susan, this is Sarah.

SUSAN: Hello.

SARAH: *(Moves over and hugs* SUSAN, *inadvertently pinning* SUSAN's *arms to her side.* SARAH *has a slight gamey odor, and* SUSAN *reacts to it.)* I've heard so much about you.

SUSAN: Oh, well I—I wish I could say the same.

ROGER: *(Laughs)* Hi, I'm Roger. What she means is we just found out about you from your note.

SARAH: Yes, Thomas wanted to keep it a secret.

SUSAN: He did?

SARAH: He wanted to surprise you.

SUSAN: Well, he's succeeded.

SARAH: I know it must seem a little strange.

ROGER: A surprise anyway.

SARAH: It reminds me of my first out-of-body experience.

ROGER: Oh?

SARAH: I was at a friend's house at the time. She was in another room and as it turned out was having one herself.

SUSAN: Having what herself?

SARAH: An out-of-body experience.

SUSAN: I see.

SARAH: Neither of us had any idea what the other one was doing. *(Smiles)* So you can imagine our surprise as we floated past one another in the hallway.

(Only SARAH and TOMMY laugh. SARAH has a strange laugh.)

ROGER: Uh huh.

SARAH: I mean, what I mean is I can relate to your surprise at reading about me and then suddenly here I am out of the blue and in the flesh.

SUSAN: *(A beat)* Yes, I see what you mean. *(Aside to ROGER)* She's a nut! A goddamn nut!

ROGER: Well, we're happy to meet you anyway.

SARAH: *(Sincerely)* I'm so glad. *(She begins to prepare a mixture in a pot which she will then put on the stove to cook.)* I'm sorry we couldn't be here earlier to greet you. A neighbor's barn burned down this morning.

TOMMY: Yeah, we've been over there helping with the animals. A few of them were injured and the vet's out of town.

SARAH: But I told Charlie not to worry. That I have a special remedy for burns that we'd bring back with us.

TOMMY: So, now that you're here, what do you think? *(Arms spread out, indicating the cabin)* Isn't it great?!

ROGER: *(Nods)* This is a uh, a lovely place you have here.

SARAH: Thank you.

ACT ONE

SUSAN: Yes, it has a nice...homespun quality.

TOMMY: That's because Sarah's made just about everything here herself.

SUSAN: Oh really?

TOMMY: The curtains, the rug. She even built the table and chairs.

ROGER: You don't say?

SARAH: *(Embarrassed)* Yes. *(Head down)*

TOMMY: Now don't get all embarrassed. She's very modest. *(Taking her in his arms)* You're my pioneer woman.

SARAH: You're my frontier squatter.

(A long wild passionate kiss that goes on and on)

(ROGER and SUSAN look from TOMMY and SARAH and back to each other. Kiss continues. SUSAN finally clears her throat to interrupt. She has to do it twice before they hear it.)

SARAH: *(They stop kissing.)* I hope you'll be comfortable here. We're going to stay at my sister Lucille's house so you can have a little more space.

SUSAN: Oh that's not necessary. We can stay at the inn down the road.

TOMMY: No, we really don't mind. Besides, why spend the money?

SUSAN: We don't want to put you out.

TOMMY: You won't be putting us out.

SUSAN: It's unnecessary. I really think we should go to the inn.

TOMMY: *(Shouts)* YOU'RE STAYING HERE!!!

ROGER: We accept your hospitality.

TOMMY: Well *(Laughs)* it sure is good to have you guys here...I haven't seen ya in so long.

ROGER: You've been a tough man to keep track of.

SARAH: Come, why don't we all sit down for a few minutes while this simmers. *(Indicates couch. In this following section she will rummage through a rag bag and take out two torn sheets. She will tie them together [or they can be pre-tied] making one long—about twice as long, i.e. twelve foot—sheet. We will not know her intention until later.)* Oh, I see you moved the bed.

ROGER: Uh, yes. It was sort of in the middle of the room. I can move it back if you'd like.

SARAH: No, that's all right. It does make the room seem bigger this way. Besides, I can get it later.

TOMMY: Sarah's got it all marked out.

SUSAN: What marked out?

TOMMY: North. Magnetic North, actually.

SARAH: You see, when you sleep with your head facing North your circulation is improved, and you're much more open to past life information.

ROGER: Interesting. And the pyramid? It is a pyramid isn't it?

TOMMY: Yeah. Sarah just made that.

SARAH: It's supposed to focus energy and help with meditation and dream clarification.

ROGER: Does it work?

SARAH: Well...I think so. It's a little too early to tell.

SUSAN: How...interesting.

TOMMY: I know you don't believe in these things, but I've never slept better.

ROGER: *(To SARAH)* Well then, I guess the proof is in the pudding.

ACT ONE

SARAH: *(Giggles coyly)* Yes. *(Shyly ventures)* But you know, when Thomas first came here I had the hardest time sleeping. I kept having these dreams filled with weird colors and sounds in them. It took a while before we figured out that when he crashed into the porch the house pivoted. So the bed was no longer set properly.

TOMMY: But once we moved it she settled right down.

SUSAN: What do you mean you crashed into the porch?

TOMMY: That's how we met. One night I uh, I was drunk as usual. Coming up the road I took the last curve kind of wide and ended up crashing into the porch.

SUSAN: Oh Tommy.

TOMMY: Poor Sarah. *(Laughs)* She came running out in her pajamas scared half to death.

SUSAN: I wonder why?

TOMMY: I wasn't hurt or anything but it was obvious I was in no shape to drive. So she brought me inside and put me to bed. And the next morning fed me breakfast. Right after that I started rebuilding the porch. That was six weeks ago. We've been together ever since. In fact, we're never apart. We go everywhere together.

ROGER: Now there's a tale of romance for you.

SARAH: Yes, it was a mark of fate.

ROGER: *(Nodding)* Fate.

SARAH: Yes. It was really all my fault. I'd been making plans for this to happen. You see, I'm thirty years old.

SUSAN: Thirty?

SARAH: Yes.

SUSAN: Why that's my age.

SARAH: I know. So you can understand how I felt when I realized my time had come. I reached out and The

Fates heard me. It was destiny the way we met. *(Taking* TOMMY's *hand)*

TOMMY: Oh, uh. Susan. Roger. I—we'd like you to uh, be our witnesses.

SUSAN: What?!

TOMMY: Sarah and I are getting married tomorrow.

SUSAN: Tomorrow?

TOMMY: Yeah, isn't it great?

SUSAN: Well I—I don't know what to say exactly. This is so sudden I— *(To* SARAH*)* You're not, I mean you don't *have* to get married do you?

SARAH: *(Smiling)* No.

SUSAN: But, what does your family think about this?

TOMMY: Her parents are dead. Just like ours. No mother-in-law problems, eh, Rog.

SUSAN: Tommy!

SARAH: My sister Lucille thinks it's just fine.

SUSAN: I see.

TOMMY: So are you happy for us?

SUSAN: Well...I, uh—

SARAH: Thomas, give them a chance to get used to the idea.

TOMMY: Oh yeah. I guess so. But hey look, you gotta strike while the iron is hot.

SUSAN: *(To* ROGER*)* Is that what you have to do?

*(*SARAH *takes the pot off the stove to allow it to cool.)*

TOMMY: Hey I've got an idea. If you wanted to, you could be our witnesses and we could be yours.

SARAH: Thomas!

ACT ONE

TOMMY: Hell in another year or so it'll be common-law anyway.

ROGER: And misery loves company.

(Smiling, ROGER turns to SUSAN, who gives him a dirty look. He instantly sobers.)

TOMMY: *(Laughs)* It was just a thought.

ROGER: We're thinking about it, one way or another.

TOMMY: That's the spirit.

SARAH: Are you hungry? Let me get you something to eat.

SUSAN: *(She and ROGER look at each other.)* Oh, no thanks. We've already had something to eat. The uh...the bread was very good.

TOMMY: Sarah baked that this morning.

ROGER: It was very good. By the way, what uh, what kind of cheese was that?

SARAH: Muenster.

(SARAH mispronounces it "Monster". A beat, noticing ROGER and SUSAN looking at each other)

SARAH: Why, was there something wrong?

ROGER: Well, it's just— We had a strange reaction. We thought maybe there was something wrong with it.

SARAH: Really? *(Very concerned)* Let me see. *(Smells cheese)* It seems to be all right... I see you drank the wine.

ROGER: Yes, we did.

SARAH: If anything, that was probably it.

ROGER: Oh, you think so? *(Gives SUSAN an "I-told-you-so" look)*

SARAH: It's one of my sister's concoctions. We call it her weed wine.

SUSAN: Her weed wine?

SARAH: She makes it out of a blend of clover, dandelions, and crab grass.

ROGER: I told you it reminded me of a golf course!

SARAH: *(Shaking her head)* Tch, tch, tch. I'll have to tell her she's making people sick. I know when I drank some of her first batch it took me days to recover. But the second batch was fine...I'm really sorry if it made you sick.

ROGER: No it's all right, we're fine now. But I don't mind telling you it gave us quite a buzz... In fact we didn't know if we were hallucinating or— Have you ever heard any strange sort of, humming sounds up here?

SARAH: Yes.

ROGER: You have?

SARAH: In my dreams.

ROGER: Oh, I see... Well, anyway, it's real head banging stuff, eh Tommy?

TOMMY: I don't know. I've never had it. I don't drink anymore. In fact, I'm totally drug free.

SUSAN: Is that true?

TOMMY: Since I met Sarah everything in my life's changed. I don't even eat meat anymore. We're both vegetarians.

SUSAN: No meat? Not even Hershfield's Sausages?

TOMMY: Nope.

SUSAN: But that was your favorite food.

TOMMY: Yeah, well now it's Soysages. Sarah is the *best cook* in the *world*!

SUSAN: *(Feeling displaced)* I see.

ACT ONE

SARAH: Thomas is very enthusiastic.

SUSAN: Yes he is.

SARAH: He exaggerates when he's happy.

TOMMY: *(He jumps up on chair.)* The world's not big enough for the way I feel!

ROGER: Down boy, down. Sit!

TOMMY: *(Sits)* Hey, remember when we used to do that? *(He begins to act like a dog, barking, etc.)* Play animals?

ROGER: No.

TOMMY: *(Barks)* Sure you do. I would be a lion or a tiger or something and you'd be a horse. *(Crawls around on the floor acting out a lion or tiger)*

ROGER: I'm afraid I don't really—

TOMMY: Sure you do! We'd play circus and I'd dress up in your brown pajamas and be an elephant and you were the ringmaster. *(Acts out elephant)*

ROGER: I'm not quite sure I—

TOMMY: Come on, you *have* to remember that!

SUSAN: Tommy, you were six years old then. Roger didn't know us until much later.

TOMMY: Are you sure?

SUSAN: Absolutely.

TOMMY: *(He is perplexed and then very angry.)* CHRIST!!! I could've sworn that— Well anyway. *(Laughs)* I guess all those years of drugs have taken their toll! *(Upset, he moves off to one side.)*

ROGER: *(A look passes between him and* SUSAN. *He moves over to* TOMMY.*)* Hey, maybe we didn't play animals but we certainly had our share of games, huh?

*(*TOMMY *pushes* ROGER *away.)*

SARAH: Now Thomas, don't be upset. *(She moves quickly to him.)* You have all this wonderful energy—He does you know—. It's just misguided, that's all.

TOMMY: *(Sulking)* Yeah yeah, I know.

SARAH: He has a special gift. He's one of the most alive persons I know. His aura is a yellow-green and very strong.

TOMMY: Yeah, yeah. All this energy.

SARAH: *(Caressing him)* It's so wonderfully...potent!

(SUSAN turns away in disgust.)

SARAH: It just needs redirection, that's all.

TOMMY: She's always telling me that.

SARAH: *(Fixing his hair)* You need reminding.

TOMMY: *(Smiles, warming up again)* I guess so.

(A beat as SARAH cuddles and rocks TOMMY. They kiss.)

SUSAN: *(Attempting to intrude)* Oh, look how hard the snow's coming down.

TOMMY: *(Crossing to window)* Yeah, they said over a foot on the radio. We'd better get going anyway. Traffic's bound to get all balled up. You about ready with that stuff?

SARAH: I think so. Here, take this.

(TOMMY takes one end of tied sheets. SARAH backs up, holding the other end until it is totally extended. ROGER is standing in the middle.)

SARAH: Do you think this is big enough to bandage a cow?

(ROGER looks from one to the other, rolls eyes.)

TOMMY: Looks good enough to me. *(To ROGER and SUSAN)* Come on, get your coats.

ROGER: Oh...okay.

ACT ONE

SUSAN: *(Softly to* ROGER*)* Wait.

SARAH: *(Pouring the liquid from the pot into a jar)* On the way back I want to stop at the food co-op and get some more tofu.

SUSAN: You know what? Maybe...would you mind terribly if we didn't go? We've been in the car all day, and I'm a little tired.

TOMMY: Don't you want to come for a ride in the truck?

SUSAN: Maybe later we could do that.

TOMMY: What about the animals? Don't you want to see the animals?

SARAH: Thomas, if they're tired let them be. You two stay here and relax. We'll be back soon. Is there anything special you'd like us to get from the food co-op?

ROGER: We're at your mercy.

SARAH: Okay. *(Waves good-bye)*

ROGER: Bye.

TOMMY: You sure you don't want to come?

ROGER: We'll see you later.

TOMMY: Okay.

SUSAN: Bye.

*(*SARAH *and* TOMMY *exit.)*

SUSAN: Well that's it! First it's drugs, then it's alcohol, and now he's brainwashed!

ROGER: "Love is blind."

SUSAN: And deaf and dumb in this case. Did you smell her hair?

ROGER: No.

SUSAN: *(About smell)* Oh my god! ...Tommy's done some pretty stupid things in his life, but this— No! I can't let this happen! We've got to figure out something before they get back.

ROGER: Susan, what the hell are you talking about? They're doing what you want us to do.

SUSAN: But you saw her. The woman is obviously crazy.

ROGER: She'd have to be to want to marry Thomas.

SUSAN: Oh shut up.

ROGER: Look, I don't think she's so bad. So her head's not screwed on too tightly. She seems to know how to handle him.

SUSAN: She treats him like a child. And what about him? Do you believe his act?

ROGER: I don't know. But the more we object the faster he'll jump into her arms.

SUSAN: They're getting married tomorrow. How much faster can he jump?

ROGER: Maybe that's why he kept it a secret. He knew we'd object.

SUSAN: Ohhhh, what are we going to do?

ROGER: I have no idea. But I'll tell you this. It'll do no good to talk to Thomas.

SUSAN: Would you stop calling him that.

ROGER: I kind of like it.

SUSAN: Well I don't. It's like we're pretending that he's somebody else.

ROGER: Maybe he is.

SUSAN: It's absurd. They're like two little kids playing house. They haven't given this any thought... Maybe

ACT ONE 35

if I have a talk with her. Maybe I can get them to put it off for a while.

ROGER: Stall for time.

SUSAN: Yes… "Strike while the iron is hot." I can just imagine what iron that is. It's ridiculous! Here you and I are trying to figure out what we're going to do. God, we don't want to make a mistake now do we? And on the other hand here's my little brother, who out of nowhere, in some grand stupid passionate gesture—

ROGER: Wait!

(Alien Sound begins softly.)

SUSAN: What?

ROGER: Shhhhh! Listen. That sound.

(ROGER crosses to SARAH. Both are near down centerstage once again.)

SUSAN: Oh no!

ROGER: It's happening again! Let's get out of here!

SUSAN: *(A step or two towards the door, but it is too late)* Roger!!!!

ROGER & SUSAN: *(Scream)* AHHHHHHHH!

(ROGER and SUSAN both are thrown this time to their knees. The transition is much quicker this time. Alien Sound reduces to a low hum.)

DEE: Enn.

ENN: Dee.

DEE: It was but a moment.

ENN: I think not.

DEE: *(A beat)* Yes, you are right. I detect changes. Time has elapsed.

ENN: Certainly for these beings.

DEE: Although not much.

ENN: No.

DEE: *(Breathes deeply)* I feel stronger.

ENN: Our presence in this dimension is greater than before.

DEE: It must be a frequencer blockage then.

ENN: Yes, some sort of warp.

DEE: Exx is adjusting.

ENN: Forging a path.

DEE: Attempting to force us through to our intended space.

ENN: *(A beat)* We are still unrealized.

DEE: *(Voice getting stronger. Arms move about, sensing area around them.)* Enn, for a moment as we receded I experienced the sensation that—I was afraid that we might never again— *(Her eyes suddenly focus and she sees her hand pass before her face.)* —interesting.

ENN: What?

DEE: I begin to gain sight...as the numbness dissipates. The...environment is...interesting.

ENN: I—I have no such experience. In fact...I feel less... and less.

DEE: Enn what is it?

ENN: I...am...dissipating.

DEE: Enn! Emergency One!

DEE & ENN: *(Simultaneously.* DEE*'s voice is louder than* ENN*'s.)* Within without, Chaos about, Connect within, The center find, The center find, Our space definnnnnnnnnnnnnnnnnnnned...

ENN: It is no use. Exx must be splitting the images, trying to push us through, one at a time. I fear that—

ACT ONE

DEE: I am almost realized!

ENN: And I...dissipate.

DEE: *(Fear)* Enn! I feel a joining to the creature!!!

ENN: Take care.

DEE: I do not know what will happen!!!

ENN: Be...ware...I...

DEE: Enn!!!

(Sound fades to silence. Eyes wide. DEE *looks frantically about.)*

*(*ROGER *groans.)*

SUSAN: *(*DEE *closes eyes.* SUSAN *groans.)* God...so...hot.

ROGER: *(Gets up, recovering faster than before. Goes for water.)* Are you all right?

SUSAN: *(Sitting up)* Water. Hurry. *(We see* DEE's *presence coming out. She looks strangely at her hands and arms, etc. Then, shaking head, it is now* SUSAN *looking at her outstretched arms thinking, "What are these doing out like this?" Etc.)*

ROGER: Here.

SUSAN: *(Gulps down water)* More. *(Looks at water glass as* DEE*)*

ROGER: Are you okay?

SUSAN: What?

*(*ROGER *helps* SUSAN *up.)*

SUSAN: God, I feel like I'm going to pass out or something.

ROGER: Maybe you should sit down.

*(*ROGER *brings* SUSAN *to couch.)*

SUSAN: Bring me another glass of water.

ROGER: All right.

(DEE *appears.*)

ROGER: Put your head down between your legs.

(*It is* DEE *whose head* ROGER *slowly pushes down. We see her eyes get wider as she goes down.*)

ROGER: That's right. (*Gets water*)

SUSAN: (*Head pops up,* DEE *looks around. Head back down*) What do you think happened?

ROGER: (*With water*) I don't know, but I don't think it was the wine this time. Here. Maybe we're dreaming. Or maybe the Army is testing some new kind of weapon.

SUSAN: I feel very strange. (*Jumps up*) Is there someone else here?!

ROGER: What are you talking about?

SUSAN: I don't know. I feel like someone's watching me.

ROGER: Come and sit down.

(*While* ROGER *speaks we see different mannerisms in* SUSAN *that suggest* DEE *coming out, e.g., her legs begin to move of their own accord. Her hand might reach out and touch her face. She fights it back with the other hand, etc.*)

ROGER: Look, I don't think we hallucinated or if we did something made us do it. I mean, people usually don't hallucinate the very same thing, unless this is some sort of rare disease.

SUSAN: Do you think we're going crazy?

ROGER: I don't know.

SUSAN: I really feel strange...Roger, I'm scared! I don't feel right at all.

ROGER: Maybe I should call the hospital and speak to a doctor. Maybe there's some kind of virus going around. (*Goes to phone*)

ACT ONE

DEE: Do not be afraid.

ROGER: I'm not.

SUSAN: WHAT!!!

ROGER: I'm okay.

SUSAN: No! I mean you don't understand. I-I-I just talked to myself!!!

ROGER: Big deal. I do that all the time.

SUSAN: No no no, you don't understand.

ROGER: Hey, are you all right? *(Touches her head)* God, you're burning up.

DEE: Try to relax.

SUSAN: AHHHHHHHHH!!!

ROGER: What?

SUSAN: *(Runs to mirror—feels face, etc.)* Who—what's happening?!

DEE: You must relax. Accommodation is essential for survival.

SUSAN: Something's inside me! It's inside of me!!!!

ROGER: Susan, stop! *(Grabbing her)* You've got a fever or something. Look at me. LOOK AT ME!

DEE: Greetings.

ROGER: What?!

SUSAN: Roger, I didn't say that. You've got to believe me. There's something else inside me. I don't know I—I feel faint.

ROGER: *(Bringing her to couch)* Honey, you've got to sit down. I'll get you some more water. *(Goes to sink. Brings back wash cloth.)*

DEE: She must reduce disturbance or damage may occur.

ROGER: Susan, you're talking gibberish. Just relax.

SUSAN: Roger, I didn't say that before.

ROGER: No of course not.

SUSAN: Words keep coming out of my mouth but I'm hearing them for the first time, just as you are.

ROGER: Uh huh.

SUSAN: You've got to believe me!

ROGER: Shhhh. *(Gently places wash cloth on her forehead and holds it there)* Feel good?

SUSAN: Better.

DEE: *(She places her hand on top of ROGER's. She is much stronger than SUSAN and ROGER tries, but is unable, to remove his hand.)* It does help. We must accommodate for we are intertwined.

SUSAN: Oh my god, did you hear that?! HELPPPPPPPPP!

ROGER: That's it! I'm calling the hospital. *(Runs to phone. Dials Information.)*

DEE: It will do no good.

ROGER: Susan, I know what's best for you. Operator, give me the number of the nearest hospital... We're in Brattleboro.

DEE: It will do no good to announce our presence.

ROGER: 555-2100. Thank you. *(Hangs up and dials)* I'll have them send the first aid squad. *(Dials)*

DEE: Interference from outside sources could be detrimental to both of us!

SUSAN: *(Moving towards him, not of her own free will. Her legs are DEE, her top half SUSAN. It is a sideways cross. Right leg scissors far across the left leg, pulling the rest of her body towards him.)* Roger! Roger!

ACT ONE

ROGER: It's okay honey, we'll get somebody over here right away.

DEE: It must be prevented!

ROGER: Hello, this is an emergency.

DEE: STOP!

(DEE *stops within a few feet of* ROGER *and waves her hand—accompanied by wavering sound—and he is sent twirling across the room. She then hugs herself as if physically restraining herself.*)

DEE: You must also stop!

ROGER: How, how did you do that?!

SUSAN: I'm not doing it!

DEE: LISTEN! Your fear is understandable, but it must be contained.

ROGER: What?

DEE: Be still both of you!

ROGER: Both of us?

SUSAN: Who are, I mean where are you—I mean I—

DEE: I am within you.

SUSAN: I know. (*Near tears*)

ROGER: Susan, what is this?

SUSAN: Roger, listen to me. I-am-not-talking!

ROGER: Well who then?

DEE: I am.

ROGER: And who are you?

DEE: I am…a traveler.

ROGER: This is crazy.

SUSAN: Will you shut up and listen!

DEE: It is good advice.

ROGER: Well go ahead. What do you want to tell me?

SUSAN: *(Gestures with hand)* Us!

ROGER: Us.

DEE: Although I am within this...person you know. I am from another...place.

ROGER: Let me guess, a monster from the id?

SUSAN: Shut up!

DEE: An entity from another dimension. We did not intend to...stop here.

ROGER: We? You telling me there's more than one of you?

DEE: We intended realization in the tenth dimension.

ROGER: I thought there were only four.

(During this next section DEE *moves towards* ROGER. ROGER *backs away and a kind of chase scene occurs.* DEE *picks up objects along the way, trying to understand their meaning. Eventually she comes to an axe which she lifts up.* ROGER *thinks she means to use it on him. He backs up over the sofa.* DEE, *realizing the axe is scaring him, drops it and then backs up over the sofa just as she'd seen* ROGER *do. She now begins to mimic everything* ROGER *does in a desperate attempt to learn how to be more like him.)*

DEE: There is a theory that everything is structurally related. That there are links through all dimensions. You are shadows of us. Layer upon layer. Worlds atop worlds. We intended only to pass through your dimension. But a functional problem has arisen, and we are deposited here, into that matter which most resembles our own...that is to say, you.

ROGER: What are you talking about? *(He begins to pick up on her imitating him and a kind of "Simon-says" situation develops.)*

ACT ONE

DEE: Physical travel interdimensionally is not possible. However, a kind of psychic travel is. In this dimension we concurrently occupy the same space.

ROGER: Who is we?

DEE: Enn was here, although not now. *(Looks up)* I am concerned. *(A beat)* It is not known how long we will be here...or if we will survive. We did not intend for this to happen.

ROGER: You mean this is a mistake?

DEE: An unforeseen occurrence.

ROGER: A mistake! That noise, that humming sound!

DEE: Is associated with the process of our arrival.

SUSAN: But what's happening?

DEE: Exx is attempting to free us from this dimension. For together we are incompatible.

ROGER: What do you mean?

DEE: We have no wish to remain in your world. It is... primitive. Also, the heat generated by our presence is causing your bodies to slowly burn up.

ROGER: You mean this is dangerous?

DEE: Continued exposure could lead to...problems.

SUSAN: *(Scared)* What sort of problems?

DEE: Your body currently supports us both. If it fails to nourish, so do we both fail. Do not be alarmed. We will do all we can to prevent it. Your body is strong and adaptive. So far no damage has occurred to either you or your replication.

ROGER: Her what?

DEE: Her replication. Her progeny. The being within not yet born.

ROGER: You mean she's pregnant?

DEE: Yes.

ROGER: What?!

SUSAN: Oh, I didn't want to tell you. *(She sits down on couch.)*

ROGER: For how long?

(ROGER *moves in behind couch. As* DEE *comes out she turns left.* ROGER *moves left to get eye contact. She goes back into* SUSAN, *turning right. He has to move right to maintain eye contact. And so it goes, moving back and forth, as* DEE *comes out between the lines, until the punch line of being alone.)*

SUSAN: About two months.

ROGER: You mean you've been pregnant all this time and you didn't tell me?

SUSAN: I didn't want it to cloud the issue.

ROGER: And if we broke up, what would you have done?

SUSAN: I would have done whatever I decided to do.

ROGER: Without consulting me?

SUSAN: No.

ROGER: Without asking me what I felt?

SUSAN: I would've known what you felt!

ROGER: Not about this!

SUSAN: Can we talk about this when we're alone?

DEE: *(She is dizzy.)* Please…do not create disturbance. Ohhhhh.

ROGER: What's the matter?

DEE: I—I am not suited to the strong currents of another.

ACT ONE 45

SUSAN: *(Feeling dizzy herself)* I'm sorry. I—I'm feeling dizzy too.

ROGER: Susan are you okay?

SUSAN: I don't know. Oh Roger, I'm frightened.

ROGER: Come and sit. I'm sorry...

SUSAN: Is there anything we can do?

DEE: It is essential that we try and accommodate. *(She stands.)* You must relax the boundaries between us. Stop fighting. Any disturbance creates differentiation, friction, and heat. We must...accept one another. *(Chantlike)* Being less, becoming more... Close your eyes. Let us adjust... Being less, becoming more. I am the length and breadth of thee.

SUSAN: *(Eyes closed)* I feel you inside of me.

DEE: *(Eyes open)* Together we merge. The boundaries ease.

SUSAN: *(Eyes closed)* Together we merge. Disturbances cease.

DEE: *(Eyes open)* Together we ease.

SUSAN: *(Eyes closed)* Together we—

DEE: —breathe.

SUSAN: As one—

DEE: —another. *(She pauses for a moment and then begins to go through a T'ai Chi-like exercise to orient herself physically to the surroundings.)*

ROGER: Susan...Susan?!

DEE: She is folded within her mind.

ROGER: She's what?

DEE: Her mind roves along its own path.

ROGER: You mean she's sleeping?

DEE: Yes.

ROGER: I guess that's good, right?

DEE: It has an easing tone to the system.

ROGER: I see. I—uh, say, what's her—I mean, what's your name. I mean do you have one?

DEE: Dee.

ROGER: Dee?

DEE: Dee.

ROGER: Dee. Hi, I'm Roger.

(ROGER *extends hand to shake.* DEE *does not shake but rather examines it.*)

DEE: Greetings.

ROGER: Will everything be all right?

DEE: Without sufficient experience, we can only surmise. *(Having completed her exercises she continues her investigation and moves about touching everything, perhaps even does something rather strange to punctuate* ROGER's *next line.)*

ROGER: I see. Okay… So, you're from another… dimension?

DEE: Yes.

ROGER: Do you look the same as we do?

DEE: There are similarities.

ROGER: Oh yeah?

DEE: But mostly differences.

ROGER: Oh, I see… Uh, what are you doing?

DEE: Survival technique. "Familiarize self with immediate environment."

ACT ONE

(ROGER *follows* DEE *about. She might create a little havoc touching things—perhaps spills water or holds knife in a dangerous way, forcing him to respond, etc.)*

ROGER: So, what does it feel like, being in another person's body?

DEE: *(She holds out hands, presses them together, and intertwines her fingers.)*

ROGER: Can you read Susan's mind?

DEE: I know only its outward course. But the longer together the more complete the interaction might become.

ROGER: So she knows your "outward course"?

DEE: She is just now opening herself up to that possibility. It is a learned process.

ROGER: You seem to be pretty interested in all these things.

DEE: The textures are familiar but the structural functions are very interesting.

ROGER: Yes, I've thought that on occasion.

DEE: You are prodigious tool makers.

ROGER: Actually I'm a writer.

DEE: An interesting array of devices used to adapt environment to self purposes.

(Sound cue: A worrisome shaking sound. DEE *begins to shake and is distracted.)*

ROGER: Hey, are you all right?

DEE: *(Unsure)* Yes. Why?

ROGER: You seem a little, I don't know, shaky or nervous. Are you scared?

DEE: *(A beat as she studies him. Then a sudden flood of emotion.)* YES!!! *(She tries to get a hold of herself.)* It is a difficult experience for both of us.

ROGER: You have regular emotions too?

DEE: *(Shaking increases)* There are...similarities.

ROGER: What's the matter?

DEE: I think I—the shock may be—I must focus! I must relax! I must not worry. I must not think of Enn. I must concentrate! I—I must—

ROGER: Would you like me to hold you?

DEE: Hold me?

ROGER: When people in our world are upset, sometimes it helps to be held.

DEE: *(Nods)* Proceed.

ROGER: *(Puts arms around her. Hers stay at her side.)* Shhhh. Stay clam. Put your arms around me...that's right. Now relax. Everything will be okay.

DEE: It...has a...solidifying effect.

ROGER: Soothing.

DEE: Soothing. You are very kind.

ROGER: Shhhh, just relax.

DEE: It has an easing quality, this physical act.

ROGER: Uh huh.

DEE: You are very sensitive. Is this the way of your kind?

ROGER: Most of us.

(DEE *begins to move away.*)

ROGER: You're feeling less afraid?

ACT ONE 49

DEE: Yes. *(She feels her arms.)* The shaking is almost gone. *(Feeling her breasts)* These body parts are... interesting.

ROGER: *(Smiles and nods)* Yes, I think so too.

DEE: They are very...sensitive to the touch.

ROGER: I know.

DEE: Your bodies are so...different.

ROGER: Oh really?

DEE: Yes. Will you...hold me again?

ROGER: All right.

DEE: Yes, there is something soothing about this process. And yet *(Rubbing her chest against his from side to side)* something arousing.

ROGER: Yes.

DEE: With your arms around me I feel...content.

ROGER: *(Puzzled)* Dee, I—I feel very attracted to you.

DEE: To be externally defined by this holding is... pleasurable. Define me.

(ROGER goes to hug DEE again. In this section she, with her superior strength, manhandles him. Perhaps she bends his head all the way back or twists it into odd positions, exploring this act in all sorts of "alien" ways—the crazier the better. No matter what she does, ROGER loves this aggressive female attention.)

ROGER: Oh yes, you feel so good! Dee, there's something happening here! I don't know what it is but I feel myself being drawn to you in a way I've never felt before.

DEE: Yes, there is something. I also feel it.

(DEE takes ROGER's head—he bends down at the waist— and rubs it across her chest.)

ROGER: You do?

DEE: An attraction. A physical tugging.

ROGER: Yes, but there is something else too. I can't put my finger on it but—

DEE: Are you not drawn to Susan?

ROGER: Of course, but—

DEE: There is your answer.

ROGER: Yes, but not like this. It's…different somehow… You think that's all there is to it?

DEE: *(Nods)* I am…not sure. I— *(She studies* ROGER.*)* There is something…special here…but I can not quite seem to— *(Suddenly contracts. Her hand covers his face. She holds him out at arm's length.)* Ooooooo!

ROGER: What is it?

DEE: A moment. *(Straightens up)*

ROGER: Are you in pain?

DEE: It subsides…she awakens.

SUSAN: Roger?

ROGER: *(Runs clear across to the other side of room)* I'm right here.

SUSAN: Oh. I was sleeping or dreaming like I was walking in my sleep.

ROGER: I know. I—Dee and I were talking.

SUSAN: What, what did she say?

ROGER: You don't remember?

SUSAN: *(Shakes head no)* I was sleeping.

ROGER: You were, I mean she was just talking about things. She's probably as scared about this as you are— as, as we all are.

ACT ONE 51

SUSAN: *(Nods)* Oh, this must be so confusing for you. First I'm me and then I'm somebody else.

ROGER: Yes, but it's—in a way it, it's sort of interesting. I— *(Getting turned on as he realizes the implications)* Are you feeling all right? *(Kisses her cheek)*

SUSAN: I'm not sure. This is very disorienting. And I—I sort of feel turned on. *(Kisses him)*

ROGER: I know what you mean.

*(*ROGER *kisses* SUSAN. *For the next few lines, FOR STAGING PURPOSES, to help define the separate roles and add variety and humor:* ROGER's *back is to the audience.* SUSAN/DEE *face him and therefore the audience. If the actress leans far out to the right side of* ROGER *she is* DEE. *Leaning to the far left side she is* SUSAN, *and so it goes back and forth.)*

SUSAN: *(Kiss again)* Do you think we should be doing this now?

ROGER: I don't know. Dee, what do you think?

DEE: It has an interesting effect.

ROGER: Dee, is this how you express affection?

*(*ROGER *tries to kiss* DEE *but* SUSAN *interrupts, swinging back to the other side.)*

SUSAN: Roger!

ROGER: Just a little scientific curiosity.

SUSAN: More than that I'd say.

ROGER: Well I can't help it if you turn me on.

SUSAN: Me or her?

ROGER: Look, you have to admit that if I ever wanted to be with two women at the same time, I could never be more faithful.

SUSAN: You're ridiculous.

DEE: Do that again.

ROGER: Huh?

DEE: Touch your lips to mine.

(ROGER *tries to kiss her again but at the last moment* SUSAN *swings back to the other side.*)

SUSAN: Roger, I don't think this is wise.

ROGER: Well—

DEE: I would like to feel that again.

ROGER: Susan, what do you want me to do?

DEE: Please?... Define me!

(ROGER *tries to kiss her once more but* SUSAN *swings back around at the last moment.*)

SUSAN: Oh I don't know. *(Pushing away)*

ROGER: You can't tell me that you're not affected by this too.

SUSAN: Well.

ROGER: Hey, I know it's really you.

SUSAN: *(Giving way)* Are you sure?

(ROGER *nods.*)

SUSAN: Well, all right.

(ROGER *and* SUSAN *kiss.*)

DEE: This touching of the lips. I feel it throughout the system. It is quite...wonderful. *(She pulls* ROGER *to her. A gentle kiss. Then a harder kiss and finally an intense, passionate one. It continues on for a bit when suddenly* DEE *jerks her head back. Her arms spread wide apart.)* It... begins.

ROGER: What?

SUSAN: I don't know. She's—if I close my eyes I can... feel her, listening? She's being...called?

ACT ONE

(Alien Sound)

DEE: Called! *(She moves violently backwards.)*

SUSAN: Roger!

*(*ROGER *rushes forward. Alien Sound intensifies.* SUSAN *contorts, etc.* ROGER *then begins to shake. Both are thrown onto the floor.* SUSAN *faces audience.* ROGER's *back is to the audience. Frozen as before, Alien Sound off. They slowly revive.* SUSAN *groans.)* Ohhhhh.

ROGER: *(Groans)* Ohhhhh.

SUSAN: *(Getting up)* I feel *(Feels self)* ...free.

ROGER: *(Sits up, back to audience. Groans.)* Ohhhhh.

SUSAN: *(Goes to mirror)* I don't feel her anymore! No, nothing! She's gone! I'm still so thirsty. *(Crosses to sink)* Are you okay?

ROGER: Yes. *(Turns quickly around to audience. Looks frantically around as he is now* ENN.*)*

SUSAN: You want some water?

ROGER: Yes, I—I feel sort of funny.

SUSAN: What do you mean?

ROGER: I don't know. Where's Dee?

ENN: *(Deep resounding voice)* Dee?!

ROGER: *(Panic!)* What?!!!

SUSAN: Oh no!

(Blackout)

END OF ACT ONE

ACT TWO

(Note: As a way of bringing some contrast and additional humor to the aliens, ENN should be thought of as being somewhat clumsy. Where DEE is very much in control, he is less successful. In short, he is a klutz.)

(In this act there is a nonverbal story being told as well. Now that SUSAN has been "inhabited", she has a heightened awareness of ENN. He also has a heightened awareness of her. Specific moments will be noted: Some for humor, some for plot advancement.)

(Stage is dark. Opening music fades into sustained high "C" chord as actors' voices are heard replaying the end of the last scene in the dark.)

SUSAN: *(Lights are out. Voice only:)* I feel...free!

(ROGER moans.)

SUSAN: I don't feel her anymore! ...Are you okay?

ROGER: I—I feel sort of funny.

(High-pitched beeping sound to help recapture tension of ACT ONE)

SUSAN: What do you mean?

ROGER: I don't know. Where's Dee?

ENN: *(Deep resounding voice)* Dee?!

ROGER: *(Panic!)* What?!!!

SUSAN: Oh no!

(Lights up/music off)

ROGER: *(Rushes to mirror)* Oh my god. It's in me!

ENN: Do not be afraid.

ROGER: AHHHHHHHH!!!!

SUSAN: Roger. Roger, stop. It's in you now. Try and relax. I know it's a shock. But you've got to calm yourself.

ROGER: You know I've never been good with physical problems.

SUSAN: I know. But you must relax.

ENN: It is equally difficult for us. We apologize for the imposition.

ROGER: You mean impossession! *(Hysteria setting in)* You know this, this, this is trespassing. It's against the law. And I don't, I can't believe that—

SUSAN: *(Pulling him over to the couch)* Come and sit down. Oh, you're burning up. I'll get a wash cloth. *(She rushes to the sink and gets a wash cloth.)*

ROGER: *(Groans)* Oh god, what are we going to do? What if this can cause cancer or something?!

(SUSAN returns and sponges his face.)

SUSAN: Roger, stop it. You're getting yourself all worked up. Here, does that feel better?

ENN: It has a cooling effect.

SUSAN: *(Startled)* Oh!

ENN: You spoke of Dee.

SUSAN: *(Timid, somewhat fearful)* Yes. You're the other one aren't you?

ENN: I am Enn.

ROGER: This is worse than throwing up.

ACT TWO

SUSAN: Enn? *(I.E., Yes! Somehow I know that.)*

ENN: Do not be afraid.

SUSAN: I'm not exactly. I—if I close my eyes I almost know you somehow.

ENN: She was within you?

SUSAN: Yes.

ENN: And she was all right?

SUSAN: She was scared like all of us. I mean we don't really know what she's like, but she seemed okay.

ENN: Good…I was, concerned.

ROGER: *(Bending over in pain)* Oooooooo! Susan!

SUSAN: It's okay, I'm right here.

ROGER: I don't like this one bit.

SUSAN: Take deep breaths. That's right. Easy now.

ENN: It is…discomforting.

ROGER: You're telling me?

ENN: I am telling you?

ROGER: This is the strangest damn thing talking to myself like this… You know you're doing this against our will.

SUSAN: *(Calming)* Roger, I think he knows.

ENN: Yes, it is also against our will. Dee has explained it?

SUSAN: Yes. We understand.

ROGER: But we don't like it. We, uh, we…

(ROGER *becomes dizzy and falls in slow motion.* SUSAN *catches him and steadies him.)*

SUSAN: *(Concerned)* Roger? Enn?

ENN: Yes, we are sorry for the...confusion. *(He begins to move about the room touching objects, trying to orient himself to the environment.)*

SUSAN: It is...confusing. *(She hugs herself, wondering about this physical sense of ENN that is growing within her body.)* You and Dee are, very close aren't you?

ENN: *(Turning to her)* Dee is my life partner.

SUSAN: You mean you're married?

ENN: We are bonded for life.

SUSAN: Oh, I see.

ENN: And you and...Roger. You are...married?

SUSAN: Well, not exactly.

ROGER: Oh let's not go into this now.

SUSAN: No, we're not.

ENN: Yet you are in sympathy with one another.

SUSAN: Sometimes.

ENN: A source of conflict. We did not mean to interfere.

SUSAN: You're not.

ROGER: *(Moans)*...Enn. I—I'm really starting to feel tired.

SUSAN: That's how I felt.

ENN: Possibly an effect of the accommodation.

ROGER: My head is buzzing.

ENN: You are— *(A beat as he "listens" internally to what ROGER is feeling)* —feeling overwhelmed. We must try to ease the tension between us.

ROGER: All right.

ENN: Close your eyes.

ROGER: Okay. *(He does.)*

ACT TWO

ENN: Good. Let us adjust. We must accept one another. *(A chant)* Being less, becoming more. I am the length and breadth of thee. *(In this following section* SUSAN *begins to mimic very slightly* ENN's *body motions. It is a sense memory, an unconscious response of her body.)*

ROGER: *(Eyes closed)* I see you inside of me.

ENN: *(Eyes open)* Together we merge, the boundaries ease.

ROGER: *(Eyes closed)* Together we merge, disturbances cease.

ENN: *(Eyes open)* Together we—

ROGER: *(Eyes closed)* —merge.

ENN: *(Eyes open)* And reemerge—

ROGER: *(Eyes closed)* —as one—

ENN: *(Eyes open)* —another… He is asleep.

SUSAN: *(Distracted)* That happened to me. *(Feeling quite strongly now the presence of* ENN *within her)*

ENN: It is good. *(Continues his search about the room)* By reducing the intake of outside stimulus the body is able to readjust.

SUSAN: I see. I…I—

ENN: *(Turning to her)* You…are secure?

SUSAN: Huh? Oh, yes. I'm fine.

ENN: …You are distressed.

SUSAN: Well I— This isn't your normal everyday occurrence you know.

ENN: No.

SUSAN: I'll be all right in a minute.

ENN: I must continue to investigate. *(He examines everything. He can cause all sorts of mishaps—perhaps he opens a draw or door and then closes it on his finger. He can get locked in a closet or the bathroom, etc.)*

SUSAN: What are you doing?

ENN: I must understand whether something can be done.

SUSAN: What do you mean?

ENN: A warp has occurred in space or time and led us to this place. I must determine whether anything exists in this dimension which we might make use of to help rectify the problem.

SUSAN: I see. Is there anything we can do to help?

ENN: No, the problem is ours to solve... *(Picking up something innocuous such as a toy stuffed animal)* And from what I see so far *(Sadly)*, I am afraid Exx will have to do it alone.

(A beat. ENN goes on to finish his investigations. SUSAN is drawn to him but holds herself back.)

ENN: ...However, these things are of interest... *(He takes a magnet off refrigerator and tries to stick it to himself. Then tries to lift refrigerator, fails, applies the same force to some pots or pans which go flying out of his hands, etc. All sorts of humor can be found with kitchen objects and appliances. Invention is the name of the game throughout this section.)* In my world I am very much interested in structural relationships. How things are put together. How they interrelate with other things.

SUSAN: I know that. I mean as you tell me it confirms what I already seem to know!

ENN: To share space is to share many things... All not so apparent.

SUSAN: I just have this strange sensation... Are you—I mean I wonder if you're feeling the same thing?

ACT TWO

ENN: Yes! These sensations are strange! *(Analyzes his own reactions while he continues picking up different objects)*

SUSAN: I don't mean all of them... Of course this is all new for you, but—Enn! My body! It seems to have a mind of its own. I can't describe it but it's reacting to you.

ENN: *(He comes finally to a large pine cone or some other phallic object, which he holds in a vaguely suggestive manner. This is neither a graphic nor pornographic act, but rather the suggestion of an innocent discovering a new part of himself.)* Yes, I think...I also feel something... It is unexpected.

SUSAN: There is something about you...

ENN: *(Speaking to self)* An attraction—

SUSAN: ...I don't understand what, that reaches out to me.

ENN: —A connection! Some sort of interrelationship! Hmmmmm, very odd. I wonder...

SUSAN: I mean I—I don't know what you must think of me.

ENN: I think, I am also...attracted.

SUSAN: You are?

ENN: There is in you, something familiar, yet something unknown. It beckons me.

SUSAN: *(Nods)* ...I'm, I'm finding it hard to resist you.

ENN: And I... *(Surprised by the following reaction)* have an irresistible urge... *(Questions reaction)* ...to confirm this with physical contact? *(Reaches out to her)*

SUSAN: Enn.

(SUSAN puts ENN's hands awkwardly on her shoulders.)

ENN: There is a strong physical response surging through this body!

SUSAN: Will you, kiss me?

ENN: Kiss you?

SUSAN: Like this.

(Mounting passion. ENN does not know how to kiss and just stands there.)

SUSAN: Yes! Oh it's so…incredible to kiss you.

(Passionate kisses on SUSAN's part. Suddenly ENN's body jerks. It is now ROGER. He shakes his head and goes right back to kissing SUSAN.) Oh Enn.

ROGER: *(Passionate)* Dee.

SUSAN: *(A beat)* Dee?

ROGER: Enn?

SUSAN: Roger?

ROGER: Susan!

SUSAN: Oh you, you woke up.

ROGER: Yes and just in time I see.

SUSAN: It's not what you're thinking.

ROGER: Oh no?

SUSAN: Scientific curiosity.

ROGER: That's not what I saw.

SUSAN: I needed reassurance! You think it's easy being here talking to you while you're asleep?

ROGER: I guess we're both finding out interesting things about each other.

SUSAN: I guess we are!

ENN: Please, do not fight on our account.

ROGER: You stay out of it!

ACT TWO

SUSAN: This has been building between us for quite some time!

ENN: I see.

ROGER: And it's none of your business!

ENN: *(Looks down sadly)* No.

SUSAN: Oh don't feel bad. I didn't mean to yell at you.

ENN: *(Head still down)* I am not...offended. It is not my place to make judgments.

SUSAN: *(Softly)* Enn?

ROGER: *(A beat)* Oh hey look, I'm sorry too. *(He extends his right hand.)* No hard feelings?

ENN: *(Shakes it with his left hand)* No...hard feelings.

ROGER: This is just so crazy. I keep half expecting to wake up. It's like I— *(Suddenly his head jerks to the side)* —What?

SUSAN: What's the matter?

(ENN looks quickly about, arms raised.)

SUSAN: Roger, what's happening?!

(Alien Sound begins.)

ROGER: He's being pulled! *(Backing up)* It's happening again!

SUSAN: Roger!

(Alien Sound up full. In this transition, which is the quickest yet, ROGER is left standing. SUSAN falls to the floor. Alien Sound stops.)

ROGER: *(Rushing over to her)* Susan! Are you okay?

SUSAN: Yes I...think—

ENN: Dee!

DEE: Enn!

ENN: At last together—

DEE: —again.

ENN: You are fit?

DEE: I am, fit.

ENN: It was…difficult—

DEE: —when we parted.

ENN: Being separate, even for a short time—I was greatly concerned.

DEE: And I.

ENN: It is a…joy to be reunited.

DEE: A joy to commune again.

ENN: How odd to address you directly in this form.

DEE: Equally odd to respond to you in it.

ROGER: I'm not sure, but I think we've just been insulted.

DEE: No offense was intended

ROGER: *(Coy)* Hello Dee.

DEE: Greetings Roger.

ROGER: I…was also concerned.

DEE: And I… Your impression has lingered. *(She touches his face with her left hand.)*

SUSAN: So, *(Pulling her left hand away with her right hand)* we're all here now, right?

ENN: Yes. A curious dilemma.

(All look at each other.)

DEE: When two become four.

ENN: Dee, have you seen this?

(Pipes under sink, or something as innocuous. Both laugh simultaneously, a short staccato laugh.)

ENN: Ha!-Ha!-Ha!—

ACT TWO

DEE: Yes, and this.

(Salt and pepper shaker? Both laugh.)

ROGER: What's so funny?

DEE: Your world is so different from ours.

ENN: The invention, the employment of mechanical principles—

DEE: —amuse us.

ENN: *(With childlike enthusiasm)* To be a thing so totally different.

DEE: *(Feeling self)* The joys that can be gotten from this body.

ENN: Yes!

(With arms straight up in the air DEE and ENN press their bodies together and roll around each other 360 degrees, like two rolling pins pressed together.)

ENN: Oh Dee!

DEE: Oh Enn! Let us press their lips to theirs!

ENN: Yes!

(DEE and ENN kiss but it is flat, monotone in nature.)

ENN: Why, it is strange kissing you. I, I think I prefer Susan.

DEE: You do?

SUSAN: He does?! *(Reaches out to touch his face)*

ROGER: Hey I'm still here, remember?

DEE: And I think I prefer Roger's lips.

ROGER: Oh yeah?

DEE: Enn, there may be more to this act than we have initiated.

ENN: Yes. I sense the need for a…horizontal plane? Perhaps we should move to the…bed?

DEE: Yes!

(Lots of fun can be had with this cross)

SUSAN: Maybe we should talk about this first.

ENN: Explanations are unnecessary.

DEE: We will do as you do.

ROGER: I'm game.

SUSAN: That's not what I meant and you know it.

ENN: *(Enthusiastically dragging* SUSAN *towards the bed)* I am also...game.

SUSAN: No, wait!

ENN: Susan, what is the matter?

SUSAN: Look, I don't mind Roger and I certainly don't mind being with you. But Dee, I sort of mind you.

ROGER: Now that she mentions it, I guess I sort of mind about Enn.

DEE: Enn, I see in Susan's mind that this act of lying down can lead to other...things.

ENN: Yes, in Roger's mind also. Especially with... Eleanore?

SUSAN: Eleanore? Who is Eleanore?!

ROGER: Oh for god's sake. She's just a character I'm trying to write.

ENN: But she is so vivid.

SUSAN: I've said before that I think the only thing that's real for Roger is his fiction.

ENN: His fiction?

SUSAN: His writing, the world he imagines.

DEE: Enn, do you hear this? It reminds me of you.

ENN: I fail to see your reasoning.

ACT TWO

DEE: You are detached in many ways.

ROGER: Oh is he now?

ENN: An exaggeration at best.

ROGER: Tell me more.

DEE: His mind is filled with speculations. He is often lost, searching for things that do not exist.

SUSAN: Roger too.

ENN: It appears, Roger, that Susan and Dee have a similar complaint.

ROGER: I write stories, Enn, I don't get lost in them.

DEE: But stories are speculations. They are tools used for searching.

ROGER: I don't know what you mean?

DEE: We remember the past but it is no longer. We anticipate the future but it has yet to come. We exist in the breakneck speed of the moment.

ENN: The stories you surround yourself with are devices for looking back on something, or forward to something. But what you live is…something else entirely.

SUSAN: Roger, are you listening to yourself?

DEE: Now Susan, do not be so hard on him.

ENN: Dee, you should not tell her what to do.

ROGER: Hey, whose side are you on anyway?

DEE: Enn, I think that Roger is more sensitive than Susan may realize.

ENN: And I see that Susan is not as overly demanding as Roger might have you believe.

DEE: Why is it that you insist on contradicting me? I think your judgment is clouded. I think you may be affected by the transition!

ENN: And what about you?! Can you freely say that your thoughts have not been colored by this intermixing?!

DEE: What do you mean?!

ENN: Listen to us. We are starting to sound like them! *(A beat)* Dee, what is distracting you?

DEE: Me?

ENN: Yes, you are...different. You are filled with a passion that ignores our reality... Do you care for this being? *(We see ROGER stand before her. She reaches out and touches his face.)*

DEE: He has certain vulnerabilities, a certain openness I admire. And you? Do you care for this being?

(We see SUSAN stand before ENN. He reaches out and touches her face.)

ENN: The intensity with which they feel biologically... is intoxicating... I—yes. There is something about her that moves me in ways I am unsure of. I reach out but cannot touch it... I feel so constrained by this body's limits. Its clumsy borders.

DEE: I long to touch, to intermingle with you as we once did.

ENN: *(Sighs)* To be so physically defined.

DEE: And yet to be so disconnected.

ENN: To be so self contained.

DEE: Yet to be so alone. I wonder, is this the isolation they must feel?

(Sound cue; all stagger.)

SUSAN: Uh, excuse me but it, it's really getting hot in here, don't you think?

ROGER: Yeah, and...I'm beginning to feel a little sick.

ACT TWO

SUSAN: Let's open the windows. *(She does.)* It's hard to breathe with both of you here.

(Sound surge; all stagger again.)

SUSAN: *(Holding stomach)* Dee!

DEE: I will peer within.

(Sound cue: As DEE "peers within" we hear the faint beat of her heart. It gets louder and louder. In the background a second baby heartbeat is heard. It gets louder, superseding her heart until we only hear the baby heartbeat.)

DEE: The progeny...is in rootbase form. Irritated but not damaged as yet. Its mental patterns are very malleable. However, it is beginning to realign itself to ours. I had better withdraw.

(Sound fades to silence)

ENN: *(Softly)* It may be of no consequence.

DEE: Enn?!

ENN: I am afraid we—

DEE: —are dying.

ROGER: What?!

DEE: If Exx cannot free us from this dimension soon... we will die here. And to our distress that will be the cause of your own deaths.

SUSAN: Oh my god!

ROGER: Wait a minute. You mean we could actually die from this?

DEE: The possibility grows with each passing moment.

ROGER: I can't believe this is happening!

ENN: Everything ends. The elements, the atoms which bind us, all dissipate eventually. It is only a matter of time.

SUSAN: But it's too soon for us to die!

DEE: To inflict you both with our fate is violation, and for that we are deeply grieved.

ROGER: But there must be something you can do! Think. Think!

ENN: I...have a theory. I believe there must be a blockage between this and the next dimension. If only we could *see* into the next dimension—

DEE: We might be able to effect a change!

ENN: Yes. But all your tools confirm only three-dimensional space.

SUSAN: What about this. *(Holding up small telescope or a magnifying glass)*

ENN: Three-dimensional.

ROGER: How about something electrical?

DEE: Three-dimensional

ROGER: Well if you can't see it, what can you do? Can, can you feel it?

DEE: Enn! Something in their cellular life?

ENN: Possibly. The shape of interdimensional space might be reflected in their organic material. But their bodies are too complex.

SUSAN: What about this? It's a plant. It's alive.

ENN: Yes, a simplified organic form! Let us observe its essence.

(They both reach out and touch-without-touching the plant, with accompanying Sound cue.)

DEE: It is difficult to...penetrate.

ENN: Our perceptions are dulled but we will have to make due... Have you memorized the molecular pattern?

DEE: As much as possible

ACT TWO

ENN: Good. Now let us reposition the plant.

(They both take a side of the pot and move it to the kitchen table.)

SUSAN: What are you doing?

ENN: If successful the molecules will realign themselves. And the difference between here

(ENN points to "here"; DEE points to "there".)

ENN: and there—

DEE: —should reveal the source of the problem.

(Both DEE and ENN point skyward. A beat. Both go back to examining the plant as before with appropriate Sound cue.)

DEE: ...There is no difference—

ENN: —as of yet. Let it sit and absorb the currents for a few moments.

(Sound surge; all stagger.)

DEE: *(Nods)* Let us also sit.

(Both sit. Then softly to ENN:)

DEE: Their ability to tolerate our presence is weakening.

ENN: Yes.

SUSAN: *(Yawns)* I'm really getting tired.

ROGER: Me too. *(Yawns)*

DEE: Their spirit withdraws.

ENN: Making more room for us. A wise choice. This mind-body has good instincts for survival. I like it more and more.

(Sound surge; both groan in pain.)

ROGER: Susan?

SUSAN: Roger?

ENN: The time draws near. Come, let us see if there is a change in the plant essence.

DEE: It is...still too soon.

ENN: But clearly a change has begun!

SUSAN: It has?

ENN: Yes! There is some rudimentary realignment. We must monitor the plant—

DEE: —to the very end.

(DEE *and* ENN *hover over the plant as before.*)

DEE: Yes, I think that it will not be very long before we—

(*Suddenly* DEE *and* ENN *both look sharply towards the door.*)

DEE: OH NO! A vehicle—

ENN: —Approaches!

DEE: Visitors! Danger!

SUSAN: What?

ENN: Visitors approach!

SUSAN: It's probably Tommy and Sarah.

ENN: Danger. Danger! (*He flaps his arms like Robbie-The-Robot from* Lost In Space.)

DEE: (*Jumping up and moving towards the door*) We must not let them in!

ENN: Yes! Barricade the door!

(DEE, *with one hand, pulls a chair over to the door.*)

SUSAN: No, wait. (*With the other hand pulls it back*) You can't do that.

ENN: Why not?

SUSAN: You don't understand. This is *their* home.

ACT TWO

ENN: We will hold them off as long as possible.

ROGER: Tommy'll get in if he has to crash through the wall with his truck.

SUSAN: Why can't they come in? What are you afraid of?

ENN: Listen carefully. We exist here psychically. The more contact with your species, the stronger the psychic bonds.

DEE: If too strong we will be held back in this dimension…to the end of all of us.

ROGER: *(Panicking)* Oh my god. What are we going to do?!

DEE: Do not panic! Control is our only hope.

ENN: Yes! You—we—you must pretend that we are not here!

DEE: Yes!

SUSAN: They'll think we're crazy.

ROGER: Sarah probably won't notice.

DEE: Act as though all were normal. We will recede as much as possible to help reduce contamination and confusion.

ENN: Tell them nothing. It is essential for all of our survival!

(Voices of TOMMY *and* SARAH *off stage)*

ENN: Come, there is no time.

*(*ENN *and* DEE *"fade away". Knock on door)*

SUSAN: Roger! I don't know if I can do this.

ROGER: *(Embracing her)* Susan, we have to hold on. I forgot how much I trusted you. We can do this together. Trust me?

*(*SUSAN *nods. Knock at door)*

ROGER: A kiss for luck.

(ROGER *and* SUSAN *kiss.*)

TOMMY: *(Knocks again)* Hey you two, it's us. Come on, open up.

ROGER: Are you ready?

SUSAN: Yes.

ROGER: Here goes nothing.

TOMMY: *(Knocks again)* Susan!

(ROGER *opens the door.*)

TOMMY: Jesus, there's a blizzard out here you know. What took you so long?

ROGER: We were…otherwise engaged.

TOMMY: Oh. *(A knowing smile)* Hey, it's freezing in here.

SARAH: All the windows are open. *(Moves to close them)*

TOMMY: What are you, crazy or something? It's fifteen degrees out.

ROGER: We wanted to smell the fresh mountain air.

TOMMY: You could've gone outside.

SARAH: Thomas is right. *(Stops and stares at them)* Are you two okay?

ROGER: We're not cold, really.

TOMMY: Not cold?

SUSAN: We've been exercising. I still feel rather warm.

SARAH: Exercising, is that what you've been doing?

ROGER: Yes. So how are the animals?

TOMMY: Fine. They're gonna be all right.

ROGER: Well, that's good to hear.

SUSAN: …Why are you staring at us like that?

ACT TWO

TOMMY: You know, ya look a little...your eyes are very bright. I didn't notice it before but you look like you've got suntans or something... And your eyes are so bright.

ROGER: Uh, yes. We—we went to one of those tanning booths before we came here. They said it would happen like this. That, that we'd keep getting darker for a while.

TOMMY: Oh.

SARAH: Is that healthy?

ROGER: We're not sure.

SARAH: It's all done with radiation, isn't it?

SUSAN: *(Panicking)* We don't know!

SARAH: I don't think it's very good for you.

ROGER: I'm sure you're right.

SUSAN: *(An awkward moment of silence)* ...Uh, can I help you with anything?

SARAH: Okay, if you wouldn't mind setting the table.

SUSAN: Fine. *(Both in kitchen)*

SARAH: Are you hungry?

ROGER: Now that you mention it, I'm starved.

SUSAN: *(Worried)* Me too.

SARAH: Well then maybe I'll start dinner a little earlier. But we can have something to snack on first.

SUSAN: Sounds fine with me.

SARAH: Would you mind opening this and putting it in that bowl?

SUSAN: All right.

(They prepare a raisins-and-nuts mix—puffed rice will do nicely. They continue action, silent conversation.)

TOMMY: Come on Rog, *(Crosses to sitting area)* I want to show you this project I'm working on. *(He pulls out a box from under the couch.)* Remember how I used to whittle all the time with that knife you gave me?

(ROGER gives TOMMY a blank look.)

TOMMY: Don't tell me you don't remember the knife?

ROGER: I remember the knife. I just wouldn't call throwing it into the basement door, whittling.

TOMMY: Yeah well, I was building up to whittling. But here, look. *(Takes out box of wooden carvings of animals. He will pull out three animals, one at a time. The first is normal:)*

ROGER: This isn't half bad. *(The second animal is a horse with a head on both ends. He reverses it several times, trying to figure it out.)*

TOMMY: I haven't painted 'em yet, of course. Right now I'm just trying to get the right combination together to sell.

ROGER: To sell?

TOMMY: Yeah. Sarah's sister Lucille has a small souvenir shop in town. She thinks they could be a real good seller. You know, carved from Vermont maple trees. We'd call em "Animaples".

ROGER: *(Nods)* Animaples.

(The third and last animal is vaguely prehistoric and monstrous. The presence of ENN might be seen to come out and examine this one.)

TOMMY: Yeah. She thinks if they take off we could sell them to other stores all over the state.

ROGER: That's...great.

(They continue to have silent conversation.)

ACT TWO

SARAH: Can you put these out? *(She hands* SUSAN *some earthenwear dishes and silverware.)*

(As SUSAN *sets the table, she suddenly stops, dish in hand, and the presence of* DEE *is seen reaching the other hand out towards the plant. She uses the dish to hide her action.* SARAH *looks at her, almost catching* DEE *in the act.)*

SARAH: Do you like them?

SUSAN: What?

SARAH: The dishes.

SUSAN: The dishes? Oh yes, of course, the dishes.

*(*SUSAN *says this too emphatically, overcompensating for nearly getting caught.* SARAH *misinterprets this as a harsh judgment and she lowers her head self-consciously.)*

SARAH: *(A beat)* Thomas, we'll need some more wood for the stove.

TOMMY: Okay.

SARAH: Why don't you and Roger go now and get some. And while you're out there, show him the work you did on the porch.

TOMMY: In the snow?

SARAH: It's all a part of the whole. *(I.E., please leave)*

TOMMY: Ohhhh. Okay, let's give the womenfolk a chance to talk. Come on. *(Goes to get coat)*

ROGER: *(His left hand—i.e.,* ENN*—grasps his collar.)* Uh! *(And leads him away to downstage area, facing audience.* ROGER *tries to cover.)* Yes, in a minute I—I just had a thought. I—I need to write it down. *(To self)* What are you doing!

ENN: *(Quietly to* ROGER*)* We must be very careful about this, Roger.

ROGER: What do you mean?

ENN: What is the location of this shed?

ROGER: Oh. *(To* TOMMY*)* Uh, do I need my coat?

TOMMY: Yeah, it's cold out.

ROGER: I mean is the shed far away?

TOMMY: It's just out back.

ROGER: How far is that?

TOMMY: About ten feet. What's the big deal?

ENN: Close enough if we have to get back quickly.

ROGER: I'm just curious, that's all.

SARAH: Thomas, don't forget your hat.

TOMMY: I don't need it.

SARAH: Come on. You don't want to catch a cold now, do you? And here, Roger, you use mine. *(Places her hat on his head)* I won't take no for an answer.

TOMMY: *(To* SUSAN*)* Okay, we'll be back soon.

(ROGER *and* SUSAN *look at each other.*)

SARAH: Susan…I hope we can be friends. Thomas has spoken so much about you. I'd really like to get to know you better.

SUSAN: Now might not be the best time.

SARAH: *(A beat)* I—I wanted you to know that I only have Thomas's best interests at heart.

SUSAN: Yes, we have that in common.

SARAH: I, I imagine you might have some questions.

SUSAN: There's…a lot on my mind right now.

SARAH: Please don't be upset. I know I'm ten years older than Thomas. And it might seem a little sudden. But I assure you what we have is as genuine as if we were seeing each other for years.

ACT TWO

SUSAN: I—I don't know if I can think about this right now.

SARAH: People can fit together like a jigsaw puzzle. It's very hard to find the correct piece, but when you do you know it's right. That's how it is with us.

SUSAN: *(Trying to focus)* But you hardly know my brother.

SARAH: I don't know all the individual parts. But I know the collective person.

SUSAN: The collective... *(Softly almost to self, i.e., to DEE:)* It's...hard to concentrate.

DEE: *(Whispers back)* You must try. Be what you would be.

SARAH: You're not feeling well, are you?

SUSAN: Just a little dizzy...that's all.

SARAH: You look like you've got a fever. *(She reaches out to touch SUSAN's forehead.)*

SUSAN: NO! DON'T TOUCH ME! I—I mean I'm fine. I'm really okay. I—I'm sorry. I didn't mean to sound so touchy. I, I think I'm a little queasy from the wine.

SARAH: Let me make you some herbal tea. I have a special blend that might help you feel better.

SUSAN: I doubt that would help.

DEE: *(Whispers)* Be what you would be. Do what you would do.

SUSAN: Well I—okay, yes. I'll have some. Thank you... You're very...caring.

SARAH: My sister Lucille says I have strong maternal instincts.

SUSAN: Yes, I can see that...I think Tommy sees you as the mother he lost.

SARAH: A little bit, probably. *(Prepares tea)*

SUSAN: And I—I think you baby him too much.

SARAH: The boy needs to be a boy, so the man can grow to be the man.

SUSAN: And what happens when the boy becomes the man?

SARAH: We all grow.

SUSAN: And leave the nest. Will he still want you then?

SARAH: *(A beat. A difficult moment for her, filled with the pathos of her life. Near tears:)* I don't know.

SUSAN: *(Sighs)* Look Sarah, I— *(Starts rubbing her forehead)* I...

DEE: You must continue. Speak as you would speak.

SUSAN: Sarah, I'm not trying to talk you out of this, but don't you think you should spend a little more time getting to know one another? ...Tommy took our parents' death very hard. It's left its impression.

SARAH: You mean his mind?

SUSAN: There's always been something...strange about him.

SARAH: Yes, he has the mark of madness on him.

SUSAN: You've seen it?

SARAH: The Indians would have said he was "touched". To be revered...and steered clear of.

SUSAN: Sarah, what can you possibly gain from this?!

SARAH: ...A kindred spirit. I, feel so alive when I'm with him. *(A beat)* He very much needs your approval.

SUSAN: ...And if I say no?

SARAH: I would hope that you wouldn't. You're too important to him. We need your understanding and your blessings. *(A beat)* If... If you think this is harmful

ACT TWO

to him. If you think we should wait. I... *(Head down in supplication, sad)* I will honor your wishes.

(A beat)

TOMMY: *(Door opens, men enter.)* We're back.

(ROGER and TOMMY put wood in bin.)

ROGER: How are you?

SUSAN: Okay.

(ENN secretly tries to reach out to the plant but is interrupted by TOMMY and quickly withdraws.)

TOMMY: So, did you two have a nice "chat"?

SARAH: Yes.

TOMMY: What did you talk about?

SARAH: *(Smiling)* None of your beeswax.

TOMMY: *(To SUSAN)* Come on, tell me.

SUSAN: Tommy.

TOMMY: I want to know. What's the big deal?

SUSAN: We talked about lots of things.

TOMMY: Like what?

SUSAN: Well, you know.

TOMMY: Hey come on Susan, if you talked about me I think I have the right to know what was said!

SARAH: *(Laughs)* Thomas likes to know everything. I think that's part of his personality. He's really very bright.

SUSAN: We've always known that.

TOMMY: *(Softening)* I think I have a right to know, that's all.

SARAH: Well, you can't know everything. Besides, it's important that Susan and I get to know one another and we can't have you butting in every five seconds.

(Smiles to ROGER *and* SUSAN*)* Now come and help me get the candlesticks.

TOMMY: The candlesticks?

SARAH: Yes. The silver ones. It's a special occasion. *(To* ROGER *and* SUSAN*)* Why don't you two have a seat. *(Moves* TOMMY *off to side where candlesticks are kept in the bottom drawer of dresser. Softly:)* I think something is wrong.

TOMMY: *(Loud)* What do you mean?

SARAH: Shhhhh.

ENN: They are growing suspicious.

*(*ENN *and* DEE *reach out to the plant through this section. Their hands remain as* ENN *and* DEE.*)*

DEE: Particularly the woman.

SARAH: I can't put my finger on it.

ROGER: How do you know that?

TOMMY: Ah, they're just mad that we're beating them to the punch.

*(*SARAH *shakes her head no.)*

SUSAN: She's right. I'm afraid I acted a little strangely.

ROGER: What do you mean?

SARAH: No, Thomas, something doesn't feel right.

*(*SARAH *silently mimes the following as* SUSAN *describes it.)*

SUSAN: She said I looked like I had a fever. She reached out to touch my forehead. I yelled at her to stop. I—

SARAH & SUSAN: *(Simultaneously)* —blamed it on the wine.

SARAH: But I don't believe her. I think she's trying to hide something. I think she might be sick.

TOMMY: Sick?

ACT TWO 83

ENN: The pattern is almost formed.

DEE: Just a little more time.

(They withdraw hands.)

TOMMY: Well, maybe I should say something.

SARAH: No, let's wait a while.

ENN: I sense an undercurrent—

DEE: —emanating from the woman.

SARAH: I've brewed her some herb tea. Maybe that will help.

ENN: She reaches out in unexpected ways.

SARAH: But I want you to watch and tell me what you think.

DEE: We must be extremely careful.

TOMMY: Okay.

ROGER: *(A big yawn)* Ohhhh. Sorry.

SARAH: *(With candlesticks)* Okay, here we are. *(Puts them on the table)* There, that looks a lot better, don't you think? (She then quickly takes the plant off the table, returning it to its original place.)

DEE: NO!!!

SARAH: What?

SUSAN: No, uh, no you're right, it's a, a very nice touch.

SARAH: Thank you.

DEE: *(Whispers)* Enn.

ENN: *(Whispers, touching hands)* Dee.

DEE & ENN: *(Simultaneously. Imploring, as if to say, "Our fate is in your hands".)* Exx!

SARAH: Now, how about a little snack?

ROGER: Well, okay. I—we are hungry.

TOMMY: Suzy, come here a minute. I want to show you my animal carvings.

SARAH: Thomas, you can do that later. They're very hungry. Let's let them have something to eat first.

TOMMY: Okay, sure.

(They all sit.)

TOMMY: So...who would've thought a year ago that I'd be sitting here at the table about to eat a dinner prepared by my wife-to-be, in the company of my family... Isn't it great?

ROGER: *(Yawns)* Very nice.

SUSAN: Yes. *(Yawns)*

TOMMY: Are you having a good time?

ROGER: So far. *(Yawns)* Sorry, I just— *(Yawns)* Suddenly I feel so tired.

SUSAN: *(Yawns)* Oh don't get me started.

DEE: *(Whispers)* Now is not the time!

ROGER: Sorry. I— *(Yawns)* If I could... just...close my... eyes for just a... *(Eyes closed, falling asleep)* for just a sec— *(His left hand comes up and pinches his cheek.)* —ond...OUCH!

(ROGER slaps his hand away. This action causes them all at table to jump.)

ROGER: I mean I, ha! I'm wide awake.

TOMMY: Roger, what are you doing?

ROGER: What do you mean?

TOMMY: Both of you. What gives? Suzy, are you sick or something?

SUSAN: Things are...hectic right now. That's all. *(Yawns)* And we're a little tired.

ACT TWO 85

ROGER: *(Yawns)* Sorry I— *(Yawns)* it must be the mountain air. I— *(Yawns)* I don't know…what's *(Eyes closing)* come…over me. I… *(Head down. He is asleep.)*

SUSAN: Roger? Roger!

ENN: *(Suddenly body jerks, eyes wide open)* Yes! I-am-Roger. I am…no longer tired.

SUSAN: *(Whispers)* Enn? *(Yawns)*

ENN: *(Whispers)* Say nothing. *(Puts on a big smile. An awkward silence ensues. He tries to cover, searching his mind for something to say.)* So…how…is, the weather?

TOMMY: The weather?! You know you both seem kind of, I don't know. Ya, you're, you're weird or something.

SUSAN: You haven't seen us for a long time. *(Yawns)* People change or you remember them differently. *(Yawns)* Oh, excuse me.

TOMMY: Still, not this much.

SUSAN: *(Yawns)* Uh, I'm sorry. *(Whispers to self)* I don't know…if…I can *(Eyes closing)*…stay…awake much lon— *(Head slowly goes down until her face is flat on her plate, asleep.)*

ENN: Susan? Susan? *(Nudges her)*

DEE: *(Head up, eyes open)* I am…refreshed.

SARAH: I think you both better eat something to give you some energy before you pass out. Thomas, hand them the bowl.

TOMMY: Sure.

(TOMMY takes a handful of the raisins and nut mix, cocks his head back, and with exaggerated style pops it into his mouth before passing the bowl onto them. DEE and ENN watch him very carefully and then try to repeat his action exactly.)

ENN: Thank you. *(Takes mix. He opens his mouth wide and tries to throw it in, but misses most of it.)*

DEE: Thank you. *(She is successful in getting it into her mouth.)*

ENN: HMMMMMMMM!

(This is the first time DEE and ENN have tasted food.)

ENN: Very good! *(Throws more into his mouth and misses much as before)*

DEE: This is...amazing!!!

(DEE takes more. She gets ENN's attention and shows him how to get the mix into his mouth.)

ENN: An unexpected...pleasure! *(He follows her lead and is successful. Eats more)*

DEE: *(Eats more)* It is so good. I could not...imagine it!

(DEE and ENN continue to eat and moan with pleasure.)

TOMMY: Didn't I tell ya Sarah was a great cook?

(DEE and ENN nod.)

SARAH: Thomas, it's raisins and nuts. I didn't cook anything.

TOMMY: Maybe it's the way you mixed them.

SARAH: Haven't you had raisins and nuts before?

ENN: *(Shakes head no)* ...I mean, of course we have. Many times... My mouth, calls for a rinsing. I am... thirsty? Yes thirsty. Can I have a glass of...water?

SARAH: Yes of course. *(Goes and gets it. Also takes out of refrigerator a tabouleh salad.)*

DEE: I also would care for some liquid.

SARAH: Drink your tea.

DEE: Oh yes, my tea.

ACT TWO 87

TOMMY: *(Seeing bowl is empty)* You guys inhaled the mix. You're really hungry, aren't you?

ENN: I think it…must be the mountain air.

TOMMY: I'll get you some more.

DEE: Thank you. That would be enjoyable. *(She then samples the tea.)* Uh! *(Surprised)* Why, why this is…hot!

SARAH: It's not too hot for you, is it?

DEE: Oh…no, it is not too hot. It, it…hits…the spot. Yes. Hmmmm. I like it very much. *(To* ENN*)* Here, try some.

TOMMY: *(Quietly to* SARAH*)* I see what you mean.

SARAH: I don't have a good feeling about this.

(Silent conversation)

DEE: *(*ENN *tastes the tea and frowns.)* What is wrong?

ENN: It is not to my liking! *(He hates the taste and sticks out his tongue which he then wipes with a napkin.)*

DEE: An interesting contradiction. Perhaps gender based?

ENN: I do not know. I think it is…not—my—cup—of—tea.

TOMMY: They drank the weed wine. Maybe that's it. Maybe there was something really wrong with it.

SARAH: I don't know. I'm getting very strange vibrations. Does the house seem stuffy to you?

TOMMY: A little now that you mention it.

SARAH: Something's going on here.

TOMMY: Like what?

SARAH: I don't know yet. I need to get into a problem-solving theta-state. I need to meditate. Give me a minute or two.

(They come back to the table. TOMMY *brings the mix.* SARAH *crosses to sitting area, sits down, and begins to rock slowly from side to side.)*

TOMMY: Here you go.

*(*DEE *and* ENN *eat with hands as before, with gusto.)*

ENN: Thank you. Hmmmmmm.

DEE: Yes. Hmmmmmm. This is...indescribably—

DEE & ENN: *(Simultaneously making the association)* — delicious!

ENN: Yes!

*(*DEE *and* ENN *continue to eat with great enthusiasm.)*

TOMMY: Yeah, well, don't fill up on that stuff.

ENN: Oh.

*(*DEE *and* ENN *both abruptly stop eating.* ENN *opens mouth wide and takes the last bit of food out of his mouth.)*

ENN: No, of course not.

DEE: Yes... Save...room for dinner.

ENN: Yes... A...penny *saved*...is a penny earned. *(Proud of self. Big smile)*

DEE: *(A beat as they search for associations to make conversation)* In for a *penny*, in for a pound.

ENN: Yes! Penny wise and *pound* foolish!!

TOMMY: What the hell is all this penny talk?

ENN: Oh! We—I was...making an association?

DEE: Yes, he was...joking.

ENN: Yes, joking.

DEE & ENN: *(Simultaneously laugh their short staccato laugh)* Ha!— Ha!-Ha!

TOMMY: Yeah, well, I never thought your jokes were very funny.

ACT TWO 89

ENN: Oh... No, they were not.

TOMMY: Look, if you're still hungry you want to have your salads now?

DEE: That would be...fine.

ENN: Yes. We would like our salads, now!

TOMMY: Okay. *(He goes and puts salad in four separate bowls.)*

(In the meantime DEE notices SARAH's slow rocking. She looks at herself and ENN, then slowly begins to rock in exact time with SARAH. She alerts ENN to do the same. Soon they are all rocking slowly in time to each other.)

TOMMY: This tabouleh salad is one of Sarah's specialties. She has her own special salad dressing that she makes using home-grown spices.

DEE: We...await...with anticipation.

ENN: Yes...we have, baited breath.

TOMMY: Huh? *(Returning with salad)* What are you two doing?

ENN: *(Both stop.)* Oh. We were...rocking.

DEE: From side...to side.

TOMMY: Yeah well don't bother her. She's trying to meditate.

DEE: Oh, yes...of course.

ENN: Yes, of course. *(He uses his hands to eat the salad—a large piece of lettuce will do—but he falls into old habits and inadvertently misses, throwing it over his head.)* Hmmmmmm!

DEE: *(She, of course, is successful in getting it into her mouth)* A wonderful texture.

TOMMY: Oh that's it! You two are definitely acting funny!

ENN: We do not intend to be humorous.

TOMMY: Roger, what the hell are you trying to do? Both of you! You think you're gonna scare Sarah away by acting crazy? Is that what you're doing?

ENN: That is not our intention.

TOMMY: You think I'm stupid or something? You think I don't know what you really think about this whole thing?

SARAH: *(Starting to come out of her meditation)* Thomas.

TOMMY: No, I'm getting mad now! You never approve of anything I ever do. You're always getting on my case.

(DEE and ENN look at each other and shrug.)

TOMMY: You think I'm still a kid. But I'm not. I'm twenty years old. I've been on my own a long time now… Ah, look, I know you're concerned. Christ, you've been my parents. I know I've done some pretty stupid things in the past. But don't you see, I've found someone I really care about, and it's changed everything. It's like I care about what happens to me now because I care what happens to her. So you can act as weird as you want. It's not going to change a thing!

ENN: *(Nods)* It is your life.

DEE: We apologize if our behavior seems a little odd. We are not feeling ourselves.

TOMMY: You still high from the wine?

ENN: Yes! That is it. We are…

DEE: …still high from the wine.

SARAH: No! *(Fully out of her meditation)* That's not it!

ENN: *(Trying to agree)* Uh no.

DEE: No.

ACT TWO 91

ENN: No, no. Perhaps it is the mountain air.

SARAH: No, *(Squinting)* your auras are...almost blinding!

ENN: I do not...see anything.

TOMMY: Hey, if Sarah says they're blinding, they're blinding!

SARAH: Something has changed here. The whole house feels different.

DEE: I see no differences.

SARAH: The air is thick.

ENN: Perhaps we should open the...window.

SARAH: The house fuller!

DEE: It appears to be the same size to me.

SARAH: And you! *(Jumps up)*

DEE: Enn, I fear the worst.

TOMMY: What?

SARAH: *(Shock and fear)* Both of you are not what you were!!! YOU ARE POSSESSED!!! *(She picks up a large crystal rock and holds it in front of her, pulling* TOMMY *behind her.)* "With this crystal we are protected by divine love and infinite intelligence so no harm will come to us."

DEE: They can not be dissuaded.

ENN: *(Sadly)* No...and already I feel a weakening—

DEE: —as they draw upon us.

TOMMY: What the hell are you talking about?!

SARAH: Thomas, stay here! "With this crystal we are protected by divine love and infinite intelligence so no harm will come to us."

ENN: Please, do not be afraid. We mean you no harm.

TOMMY: You mean us no harm?

SARAH: What form of spirit are you? Of the light; or the dark?

DEE: *(Looking at* ENN*)* Perhaps, somewhere in the middle?

ENN: Perhaps.

TOMMY: Wait a minute. You mean to tell me you're not Susan and Roger?

ENN: No, we are not.

TOMMY: If you're not them, then where the hell are they?!

ENN: They are asleep. A moment.

*(*ENN *slaps himself,* DEE *slaps herself awake.)*

ENN: Wake up!

DEE: Wake up!

*(*TOMMY *grabs kitchen knife.)*

ROGER: Uh, *(Sees* TOMMY *with knife)* what's happened?!

DEE: You fell asleep.

ENN: We are discovered.

SUSAN: On no!

ENN: It is too late for remorse.

SUSAN: What's, what's going to happen? *(Seeing* TOMMY*)* Tommy, put that down.

TOMMY: Susan? Is that you?

SUSAN: Yes, of course, now put that down.

TOMMY: Not until you tell me what's going on.

SARAH: Thomas, they are possessed.

SUSAN: In a way, but not by devils or spirits or anything like that.

ACT TWO

ROGER: By aliens.

TOMMY: Aliens?!

SUSAN: From another dimension.

ENN: Greetings, I am Enn.

DEE: Greetings, I am Dee.

ROGER: They're somehow inside of us. But they're not supposed to be here.

ENN: We currently share the same space.

TOMMY: What the hell are you talking about?!

DEE: He is more receptive to Susan, perhaps I should explain. We are the first to explore interdimensional space.

ENN: We ran several tests to establish the path but when we proceeded through, something had altered.

DEE: And we were deposited here, our escape hatch you might call it.

TOMMY: This sounds crazy to me.

SARAH: I believe them.

TOMMY: So what you're saying is that you're inside my sister and Roger?

ENN: That is correct.

TOMMY: Does it hurt?

DEE: There is some physical discomfort.

TOMMY: *(Cupping his mouth with hands)* Susan, can you hear me?

SUSAN: Yes, you don't have to shout.

TOMMY: Are you okay?

SUSAN: I—I'm very scared. *(Near tears)*

ROGER: *(Putting arms around her)* We're...we're in trouble.

TOMMY: What do you mean?

ROGER: They say there's a possibility that, that we might...die.

TOMMY: What?!

(*Suddenly a high-pitched beeping sound is heard. But only* DEE *and* ENN *can hear it.*)

DEE: Enn!

ENN: Yes I hear it. Emergency Two!

DEE & ENN: (*Simultaneously*) AcceleRATE!!!

(SARAH *and* TOMMY *freeze. Strobe light flickers on* DEE *and* ENN.)

ENN: Good, we are radiating at a thousandth of a second of their time.

DEE: The warning signal.

ENN: Yes, enough power for one last attempt.

DEE: And then—

ENN: I should never have brought you into this project.

DEE: It was a large part of your life. We are a bonded pair. I could not have let you make the journey without me.

ENN: No, I suppose not. Dee, (*Touches her face*) you are more a part of my life than I.

DEE: I...find it difficult to contemplate our end.

ENN: There is...too much to express.

DEE: The expression has been our bond, our life together.

ENN: It has been...full.

(DEE *and* ENN *touch fingertips.*)

DEE: It has been full.

(*A beat as* DEE *and* ENN *stare at one another*)

ACT TWO

ENN: *(Looking at self and* DEE*)* Dee, look at us! *(Revelation)* In this accelerated state. Look at the "us" within them! Do you see it?!!!

DEE: Yes!!!

ENN: Is it possible?

DEE: Deep inside there is resonance.

ENN: Why, they are...shadows!

DEE: Reflections.

ENN: A transmuted form—in this dimension—

DEE: —of *our* spiritual essence!

ENN: It is no wonder we are so drawn to them.

DEE: We, we are recognizable even in this stage of development.

ENN: The implications—

DEE: —are staggering!

ENN: Dee, if only we could—

(High-pitched beeping sound)

DEE: Enn.

ENN: There is no time left. We must try and focus all our energy for these last moments—

DEE: —If there is any chance.

ENN: Are you ready?

(A beat. DEE *shakes head no.)*

ENN: Nor I. Still...

*(*DEE *and* ENN *both give silent farewell and then nod.)*

ENN: Now!

DEE & ENN: *(Simultaneously)* DeceleRATE!!!

(All begin to move.)

TOMMY: You might die?!

ROGER: That's what they said. How much longer before we know?

DEE: It will not be long.

SUSAN: It won't?

ENN: *(Softly)* No.

SUSAN: *(Begins to cry)* Oh, I'm so frightened.

TOMMY: Wait a second. Why will you die? They gonna tear their way out of your chest or something?

ENN: We are not physical manifestations. Rather, our life forces are intertwined.

TOMMY: And that will kill them?

DEE: If we discharge while here our system will drain theirs of their energy.

ENN: We do not want this to happen.

TOMMY: Then do something!

ENN: We are trying.

TOMMY: Well you better try harder you son-of-a-bitch! I oughtta punch you right in the—

SUSAN: Tommy stop! You'll hit Roger!

ENN: If it were in our power to do something, we would.

(Alien Sound begins.)

SARAH: What's that sound? *(Starts looking around)*

ENN: Exx is directing all energy forward, trying to push us through to the other side.

(Sound builds throughout this section to final climax.)

SARAH: That sound is familiar.

ROGER: It's the sound of them coming and going.

(ROGER and SUSAN begin to convulse.)

ACT TWO

TOMMY: Roger! Susan! What can we do?!

SUSAN: *(Sound surge)* Ooooo!

ROGER: *(Sound surge)* Ooooo!

TOMMY: What's happening?

ROGER: Susan.

SUSAN: Give me your hand.

SARAH: It reminds me of something. *(Sits on top of the bed in lotus position)*

DEE: Enn, dispersion is setting in.

ENN: We must hold if there is any chance.

DEE: To the last possible moment.

DEE & ENN: *(Chant softly)* Connect within, the center find. The center find, our space definnnnnnnnnnnnnnnnnnnned...

TOMMY: What the hell are they doing?

SARAH: *(Chanting rapidly)* Nam-Yoho-Rengay-Kyo. Nam-Yoho-Rengay-Kyo. Nam-Yoho-Rengay-Kyo... *(Etc. Continues softly until revelation)*

TOMMY: Sarah, what the hell are you doing?

DEE & ENN: The center find, our space definnnnnnnnnnnnnnnnnnned...

(DEE continues humming over next line.)

ROGER: *(Weakly)* Susan?

ENN: The center find, our space definnnnnnnnnnnnnned. *(He continues hum over next line.)*

SUSAN: Roger?

DEE: The center find, our space definnnnnnnnnnnnnned. *(Hum continues over next line.)*

ROGER: I—I'm sorry for everything. I wish I could've made you happy.

ENN: The center find, our space definnnnnnnnnnnnnned. *(Hum continues over next line.)*

SUSAN: *(Tears)* ...I love you... And you have.

SARAH: *(A deep guttural sound)* AHHHHHHHH!

DEE & ENN: The center find, our space definnnnnnnnnnnnnnnnnnnnned... *(Humming continues)*

SARAH: My dreams! Yes! Not exactly but it's the sound of my dreams!!! Thomas, the bed!

(SARAH *tries to get off but the area around the bed is now "electrified". Sound cue:)*

SARAH: OUCH!

TOMMY: What's the matter?

SARAH: *(She tries to get off but with the same results.)* OUCH! I can't get off! It's the bed!!!

TOMMY: The bed?

SARAH: Push it back to Magnetic North!

TOMMY: Are you sure?

SARAH: DO IT!!!

TOMMY: *(He moves towards the bed, stopping just short of touching it. Sound cue:)* Ouch! The air around it, it's charged up or something.

ENN: The time...is at hand.

SARAH: Hurry! You have to do it! PUSH IT!

TOMMY: *(He reaches out but again gets "shocked".)* Ouch! I can't get near it!

SARAH: You have to do it! You have to push it back! Hurry!

(TOMMY *backs up, rolling up his sleeves. He looks once more at* ROGER *and* SUSAN.)

DEE: Farewell... Forever mine?

ENN: Forever thine!

(DEE *and* ENN *hum in unison, slowly fading as Alien Sound reaches climax.*)

TOMMY: (*Charges the bed, screaming as he "breaks" through*) YAAAAAOOOWWWWWWWW! UH! YOU SON-OF-A-BITCH!!!

SARAH: Push it!

TOMMY: RRRRRRAAAAHHHHHHHH GOD DAMN BED! You won't stop me!!!! AAARRRRRRRAAHHHH! I'm Thomas Williams and you're not going to beat me!!! You son-of-a-bitch! RRRRRAAAAHHHHHH. You're not gonna beat me! You're not gonna beat me. You're not! YOU'RE NOT!!!! It's, it's moving!

SARAH: Yes! Don't stop! Keep going! That's right! Yes, HURRY!!!

TOMMY: You won't stop me! RRRRAAAAAAAAAHHHHHHH!!!! I'm Thomas Williams, I'm Thomas Williams, I'M THOMAS WILLIAMS, I'M THOMAS WILLIAMS, I'm Thomas Williams I'm Thomas Will—

(*Bed finally in place. Tremendous flash of light—or whatever—.* TOMMY *is thrown back.* SARAH *is flat on her back on bed.* ROGER *and* SUSAN *are on the floor face down. Silence.* TOMMY *is the first to move.*)

TOMMY: ...Sarah?

(SARAH *moans.*)

TOMMY: Are you all right?

(*Bed is now normal.*)

SARAH: *(Sitting up)* Yes. You did it! You did it. *(Touching his face)*

TOMMY: I did it. *(He crosses to* ROGER.*)* Hey, Rog, I did it. I did it! What the…? Susan! *(He leaps over to her.)* Susan? *(He puts his head to her heart, hears nothing.)* Oh no. It can't be. She can't be! NOOOOOOO! Suzy. SUZY! *(He gathers her in his arms.)* Oh god don't die. Don't leave me. I—I tried as hard as I could. *(Crying)* It, it wouldn't move. Oh god!!! I'm sorry. It wouldn't move. I couldn't get it there soon enough.

SARAH: *(Getting up very slowly from the bed)* Thomas.

TOMMY: Suzy. Roger. I'm sorry. I'm so sorry.

SARAH: Thomas, ssshh…you moved the bed.

TOMMY: Oh why did this have to happen to me?!

SARAH: Oh honey, don't.

TOMMY: Why does everyone I love have to die?

SARAH: Thomas…shhhhhhhh.

TOMMY: It's not fair.

SARAH: Honey, shhhhh.

TOMMY: Do you hear me?! It's not fair!!!! *(Breaking away from her)* You stupid GODDAMN BED!!! AHHHHH!!!!

*(*TOMMY *charges the bed, lifting up one corner in a fit of rage and slams it down again. As soon as it hits floor a flash of light/sound, etc. Both* SUSAN *and* ROGER's *bodies jerk.)*

SUSAN: *(Moans)* Uhhhh…

TOMMY: Susan! Roger! They're alive! They're alive!!!! Susan. Suzy! *(Cradling her head in his lap)* Are you okay?

SUSAN: Uhhhhh…I…it felt like I was drowning.

SARAH: *(Beside* ROGER*)* How are you?

ROGER: I've been better.

ACT TWO

SARAH: Breathe deeply, both of you. Good, good. You gave us quite a scare... You're both alone?

ROGER: Yes... I—I don't feel him anymore. *(He reaches out for* SUSAN.*)* Susan, are you all right?

SUSAN: Yes.

ROGER: It's only you?

SUSAN: Yes.

(Now that ROGER *and* SUSAN *are "uninhabited" there is a void they feel, and they cling to each other for balance.)*

ROGER: We've got to stop meeting like this. *(To* SARAH *and* TOMMY*)* What happened?

TOMMY: I thought you were dead.

SUSAN: What?

TOMMY: Both of you, until I lifted the bed.

ROGER: The bed?

TOMMY: The alignment must have been off a little.

SARAH: Everything changed when Thomas moved it. The bed must have been blocking their way.

ROGER: The bed? ...You know, they said they'd made tests and everything was all right.

SUSAN: Then we came here—

ROGER: —and you moved the bed. Probably between their tests and the actual run... And your dreams—

SARAH: Were affected by their test probes.

ROGER: *(To* TOMMY*)* You know, I think you might have saved our lives.

TOMMY: Hey, I just did what Sarah told me to do.

SUSAN: *(Humble)* Sarah...what can I say? *(Reaches out and they briefly hug)*

SARAH: *(Separating.* SARAH *looks up to the heavens:)* It was the fates, you know. This whole thing has their mark on it.

SUSAN: *(Feeling her arms, to* ROGER*)* Do you think they made it?

ROGER: If we did, they must have.

SUSAN: *(Scared)* Hold me tight…tighter! With your arms around me I feel… *(Says it almost like* DEE *would)* content. I— Oh no! You don't think that—

ROGER: No no, shhhh. They're gone. I know it feels a little weird, *(Unsure)* but I think it's just a, uh, a—

ROGER & SUSAN: *(Simultaneously)* —residual affect. *(A beat. They stare at each other.)*

ROGER: …You know your eyes are…I don't think I've ever seen your eyes sparkle so brightly.

SUSAN: And yours.

*(*ROGER *and* SUSAN *embrace.)*

ROGER: Oh! You feel so alive!

*(*ROGER *kisses* SUSAN. *A long passionate embrace.* SARAH *and* TOMMY *follow suit and also begin kissing. Then suddenly* ROGER *and* SUSAN *stop and part, staying at arm's length.)*

ROGER: So what does—

SUSAN: —this mean?

ROGER: *(Nods)* Are we in love with two other beings?

SUSAN: I don't know. Roger, we let it die once. Let's not let that happen again.

ROGER: Well…I'll try—

SUSAN: —if I will?

*(*ROGER *and* SUSAN *embrace.)*

(Lights begin to fade.)

ROGER: *(Clearly, in his own voice)* Dee.

SUSAN: *(Clearly, in her own voice)* Enn.

ROGER: Forever mine?

SUSAN: Forever thine!

(Lights out)

END OF PLAY

www.ingramcontent.com/pod-product-compliance
Lightning Source LLC
Chambersburg PA
CBHW060203050426
42446CB00013B/2965